GoodFood
Delicious gifts

10 9 8 7 6 5 4

Published in 2011 by BBC Books, an imprint of Ebury Publishing
A Random House Group company

The Random House Group Limited
Reg. No. 954009

Addresses for companies within the Random House Group can be found at www.randomhouse.co.uk

A CIP catalogue record for this book is available from the British Library
The Random House Group Limited supports The Forest Stewardship Council (FSC®), the leading international forest certification organisation. Our books carrying the FSC label are printed on FSC® certified paper. FSC is the only forest certification scheme endorsed by the leading environmental organisations, including Greenpeace. Our paper procurement policy can be found
at www.randomhouse.co.uk/environment

To buy books by your favourite authors and register for offers visit www.randomhouse.co.uk

Printed and bound by Firmengruppe APPL, aprinta druck, Wemding, Germany
Colour origination by Dot Gradations Ltd, UK

Commissioning Editor: Muna Reyal
Project Editor: Joe Cottington
Designer: Annette Peppis
Production: Lucy Harrison
Picture Researcher: Gabby Harrington

ISBN: 9781849902588

Picture credits

BBC *Good Food* magazine and BBC Books would like to thank the following people for providing photos. While every effort has been made to trace and acknowledge all photographers, we should like to apologise should there be any errors or omissions.

Marie-Louise Avery p127, p131; Peter Cassidy p25, p51, p59, p63, p65, p111, p135, p149, p187, p201; Jean Cazals p27, p41, p141; Tim MacPherson p89; Gareth Morgans p99, p109, p209; David Munns p13, p15, p31, p39, p57, p95, p151, p181; Noel Murphy p167; Myles New p55, p81, p93, p101, p103, p107, p115, p119, p137, p139, p143, p189, p195; Lis Parsons p19, p21, p23, p29, p35, p45, p67, p77, p79, p85, p87, p91, p113, p121, p123, p125, p163, p165, p169, p171, p173, p175, p183, p185, p191, p193, p197, p203; Maja Smend p153, p155, p157, p159, p161; Roger Stowell p43, p69; Cameron Watt p53; Philip Webb p11, p17, p33, p37, p47, p49, p71, p73, p75, p83, p129, p133, p145, p147, p179, p199, p205, p211; Simon Wheeler p61, p177; Isobel Wield p117; Elizabeth Zeschin p97, p207

All the recipes in this book were created by the editorial team at *Good Food* and by regular contributors to BBC Magazines.

weekend

GoodFood
Delicious gifts

Editor **Sharon Brown**

BOOKS

Contents

Introduction

Nothing makes a more welcome gift for friends or family than a delicious treat you've made in your own kitchen. Be it a jar of jam or chutney, a box of chocs or a batch of cookies, something homemade is so much more thoughtful and appreciated than a shop-bought present.

When you make your own gifts, you know just what they contain – with none of the additives of many ready-made versions – and if you grow your own fruit and veg, preserves are a great way to use up excess produce, so we've included a whole chapter here for you.

We've included recipes for special occasions here too, so you can celebrate Easter, Halloween or Valentine's day in style. And if there's a wedding celebration coming up, there's a selection of wedding favours to add the finishing touches to a memorable day.

From choc-dipped macaroons to cupcakes and cookies, we've also featured some wickedly tempting presents for your chocoholic friends. And don't forget Christmas, a great time to make your own gifts and show people you really care. (You can always make a batch for yourself with some extra to give away!)

Enjoy creating these wonderful treats – and enjoying giving them, too!

Sharon

Sharon Brown
Good Food magazine

Notes and conversion tables

NOTES ON THE RECIPES
• Eggs are large in the UK and Australia and extra large in America unless stated otherwise.
• Wash fresh produce before preparation.
• Recipes contain nutritional analyses for 'sugar', which means the total sugar content including all natural sugars in the ingredients, unless otherwise stated.

OVEN TEMPERATURES

Gas	°C	°C Fan	°F	Oven temp.
¼	110	90	225	Very cool
½	120	100	250	Very cool
1	140	120	275	Cool or slow
2	150	130	300	Cool or slow
3	160	140	325	Warm
4	180	160	350	Moderate
5	190	170	375	Moderately hot
6	200	180	400	Fairly hot
7	220	200	425	Hot
8	230	210	450	Very hot
9	240	220	475	Very hot

APPROXIMATE WEIGHT CONVERSIONS
• All the recipes in this book list both imperial and metric measurements. Conversions are approximate and have been rounded up or down. Follow one set of measurements only; do not mix the two.
• Cup measurements, which are used by cooks in Australia and America, have not been listed here as they vary from ingredient to ingredient. Kitchen scales should be used to measure dry/solid ingredients.

Good Food is concerned about sustainable sourcing and animal welfare. Where possible, humanely reared meats, sustainably caught fish (see fishonline.org for further information from the Marine Conservation Society) and free-range chickens and eggs are used when recipes are originally tested.

SPOON MEASURES

Spoon measurements are level unless otherwise specified.

• 1 teaspoon (tsp) = 5ml
• 1 tablespoon (tbsp) = 15ml
• 1 Australian tablespoon = 20ml (cooks in Australia should measure 3 teaspoons where 1 tablespoon is specified in a recipe)

APPROXIMATE LIQUID CONVERSIONS

metric	imperial	AUS	US
50ml	2fl oz	¼ cup	¼ cup
125ml	4fl oz	½ cup	½ cup
175ml	6fl oz	¾ cup	¾ cup
225ml	8fl oz	1 cup	1 cup
300ml	10fl oz/½ pint	½ pint	1¼ cups
450ml	16fl oz	2 cups	2 cups/1 pint
600ml	20fl oz/1 pint	1 pint	2½ cups
1 litre	35fl oz/1¾ pints	1¾ pints	1 quart

Spiced beetroot & orange chutney

A jar of something delicious always goes down well with friends and family. To make it extra special, pack it up with a box of crackers and a tasty cheese.

TAKES 1 HOUR 20 MINUTES
- **MAKES 2KG/4LB 8OZ**

1.5kg/3lb 5oz raw beetroot, trimmed, peeled and diced (wear gloves!)

3 onions, chopped

3 eating apples, peeled and grated

zest and juice 3 oranges

2 tbsp white or yellow mustard seeds

1 tbsp coriander seeds

1 tbsp ground cloves

1 tbsp ground cinnamon

700ml/1¼ pints red wine vinegar

700g/1lb 9oz golden granulated sugar

1 In a preserving pan or your largest pan, mix together all the ingredients well. Bring to a gentle simmer then cook for 1 hour, stirring occasionally, until the chutney is thick and the beetroot tender.

2 While the chutney is cooking, sterilise your jars by running them through a short hot wash in the dishwasher, or wash them thoroughly by hand in hot soapy water, rinse, then dry in a low oven.

3 Once the chutney is ready, let it settle for 10 minutes, then carefully spoon it into the jars and seal while still hot. You can eat it straight away but it will be even better after a month. It will keep for up to 6 months in a cool, dark place. Once opened, refrigerate and eat within 2 months.

PER TBSP 48 kcals, protein 1g, carbs 12g, fat none, sat fat none, fibre 1g, sugar 11g, salt 0.04g

Green tomato chutney

If you've grown your own tomatoes, you may have some that refuse to turn red, so here's the recipe you need. The tomatoes and onions need overnight salting.

TAKES 1 HOUR 40 MINUTES, PLUS OVERNIGHT SALTING • MAKES ABOUT 3KG/6LB 8OZ

2.5kg/5lb 8oz green tomatoes
500g/1lb 2oz onions
1 rounded tbsp salt
500g/1lb 2oz sultanas
500g/1lb 2oz cooking apples
500g/1lb 2oz light muscovado sugar
1.14-litre jar spiced pickling vinegar

1 Slice the tomatoes – you can skin them if you want but it's not necessary. Finely chop the onions. Layer both in a large bowl with the salt and leave to sit overnight.

2 Next day, chop the sultanas using a large, sharp knife. Peel, core and chop the apples. Put the sugar and vinegar into a large pan and bring to the boil, stirring to dissolve the sugar. Add the sultanas and apples, and simmer for 10 minutes. Strain the tomatoes and onions in a colander (but don't rinse), then tip into the pan and return to the boil.

3 Simmer for about 1 hour, stirring occasionally, until the mixture is thick and pulpy. Wash the jars thoroughly in hot soapy water, rinse, then dry in a low oven. Transfer the chutney to the sterilised jars and cover with lids (make sure the inside of the lids are plastic coated or the vinegar will corrode the metal).

PER TBSP 34 kcals, protein 1g, carbs 9g, fat 1g, sat fat none, fibre 1g, sugar 4g, salt 0.26g

Marrow & ginger jam

This light, spicy conserve is a traditional way of using up marrows, or courgettes that have grown a bit big for their boots. It's perfect for topping buttered toast or bread.

**TAKES 1 HOUR ● MAKES ABOUT
4 × 450ML/16FL OZ JARS**
4 unwaxed lemons
1.8kg/4lb marrow, peeled and cut into
    sugar-cube-sized pieces
1.8kg/4lb jam sugar
large piece ginger, about 85g/3oz,
    peeled and shredded

1 Put a couple of saucers into the freezer. Pare the zest from the lemons with a vegetable peeler, then slice them in half and juice them. Reserve the lemon shells and pips, and tie them in a muslin bag. Put the marrow into a preserving pan with 2 tablespoons of the lemon juice, then cook on a medium heat, stirring often, until the pieces are turning translucent and soft but not mushy. Bubble off any juices before stirring in the sugar, the rest of the lemon juice and the zest, ginger and muslin bag. Stir until the sugar dissolves.

2 Wash the jars in hot soapy water, rinse, then dry in a low oven. Bring the jam to the boil, then simmer for 10–15 minutes or until the marrow has softened completely and the jam has reached setting point. To test, spoon a little on to a chilled saucer. Once cool, push it with your finger; if it wrinkles, it's ready. Pot the jam then store in a dark, cool place for a few months to mature.

PER TBSP 102 kcals, protein none, carbs 27g, fat none, sat fat none, fibre none, sugar 27g, salt none

Autumn piccalilli with pear

Nothing beats the punchy tang of homemade piccalilli – this version combines the best flavours of late-summer vegetables with the first crop of autumn pears.

TAKES 35 MINUTES, PLUS SALTING OVERNIGHT ● MAKES 5 × 450ML/ 16FL OZ JARS

2 small cauliflowers, cut into small florets
400g/14oz silverskin or pearl onions
600g/1lb 5oz courgettes, cut into small chunks (about 2cm/¾in pieces)
6 firm pears, cored, cut into small chunks
100g/4oz salt
1.7 litres/3 pints cider vinegar
finger-length piece ginger, grated
2 tbsp coriander seeds
3 tbsp brown or black mustard seeds
300g/10oz golden caster sugar
8 tbsp cornflour
5 tbsp English mustard powder
3 tsp ground turmeric

1 In a bowl, mix together the vegetables, pears and salt with 2 litres/3½ pints cold water. Cover and leave overnight.
2 The next day, drain the brine from the vegetables, rinse, then tip into a large pan with the vinegar, ginger, coriander, mustard seeds and sugar. Bring to the boil and simmer for 8-10 minutes until the veg is just tender but still with a little bite. Drain the vegetables, reserving the liquid, and set aside.
3 Wash the jars in hot soapy water, rinse, then dry in a low oven while you make the sweet mustard sauce.
4 In a large bowl, stir together the cornflour, mustard powder and turmeric, then gradually whisk in the reserved hot vinegar mix until you have a smooth, thin sauce. Return it to the pan and bubble over a low heat, stirring constantly, for 4 minutes until smooth and thickened. Stir in the veg and spoon into the sterilised jars while hot, then seal. Store in a cool, dark cupboard for 2–3 months. Refrigerate once opened.

PER SERVING 31 kcals, protein 1g, carbs 6g, fat 1g, sat fat none, fibre 1g, sugar 5g, salt 1.01g

Apple & cranberry chutney

This fruity chutney really improves with age and goes brilliantly with a selection of cheeses and cold meats. Chutneys make great homemade presents.

**TAKES 1½ HOURS ● MAKES 4 ×
450ML/16FL OZ JARS**

1kg/2lb 4oz cooking apples, peeled,
  cored and chopped into small chunks
500g/1lb 2oz eating apples, peeled,
  cored and chopped into large chunks
450g/1lb onions, sliced
50g/2oz ginger, finely chopped
1 tsp peppercorns
500g/1lb 2oz granulated sugar
250ml/9fl oz cider vinegar
500g/1lb 2oz fresh cranberries

1 Put all the ingredients except the cranberries in a large heavy-based saucepan, then gently heat, stirring, until the sugar dissolves. Bring to the boil, then reduce the heat and simmer, uncovered, for about 50 minutes, stirring regularly until the apples and onions are tender, the mixture has thickened and no watery juice remains.

2 To sterilise the jam jars, wash them thoroughly in hot soapy water, rinse, then dry in a low oven.

3 Add the cranberries to the chutney, then cook for a further 10 minutes or so until just softened but not burst. Spoon the hot chutney into the hot sterilised jars and seal. Store unopened in a cool, dark place. The chutney will keep for up to 6 months. Refrigerate once opened.

PER TBSP 35 kcals, protein none, carbs 9g, fat none, sat fat none, fibre 1g, sugar 9g, salt none

Pineapple, fig & ginger chutney

The pineapple flavour really comes through in this tangy chutney, making it a perfect accompaniment for cold meats. Make some for yourself and some for a friend.

TAKES 1 HOUR • MAKES ABOUT 1.3KG/3LB

1 large pineapple, about 1kg/2lb 4oz, or 400g/14oz prepared pineapple, roughly chopped
500g/1lb 2oz Bramley apples, peeled, cored and finely chopped
5cm/2in piece ginger, finely chopped
1 red onion, finely chopped
140g/5oz dried ready-to-eat figs, chopped
2 tsp black mustard seeds
½ tsp freshly grated nutmeg
450ml/16fl oz cider vinegar
2 tsp salt
400g/14oz light muscovado sugar

1 Tip the pineapple into a food processor, then pulse until finely chopped. Tip into a large, wide pan with the apples, ginger, onion, figs, spices, vinegar and salt. Bring to the boil, stirring, then boil for 10 minutes until the apples are softened.

2 Add the sugar, then stir to dissolve. Simmer for 20–30 minutes, stirring occasionally, until the chutney is thickened.

3 Meanwhile, sterilise the jam jars. Wash them thoroughly in hot soapy water, rinse, then dry in a low oven. Spoon the chutney into the warm, sterilised jars, seal and label. Will keep for 6 months, unopened. Store in the fridge once opened.

PER TBSP 44 kcals, protein none, carbs 11g, fat none, sat fat none, fibre 1g, sugar 11g, salt 0.21g

Easy pumpkin chutney

Chutneys add zip to a lunchtime cheeseboard. This simple recipe also works well using courgettes or marrows. Once opened, store in the fridge for up to 1 month.

TAKES 1 HOUR 5 MINUTES, PLUS OVERNIGHT SALTING • MAKES ABOUT 1.2 LITRES/2 PINTS

2.7kg/6lb pumpkin, peeled, deseeded and diced

salt

3 oranges

2 lemons

500g/1lb 2oz light muscovado sugar

600ml/1 pint cider vinegar

1 Put the pumpkin in a bowl and sprinkle liberally with salt. Toss to get it all coated, cover, and leave overnight. Drain off and discard any juices, wash the pumpkin in cold water, then drain again to remove excess moisture.

2 Peel and segment the oranges and lemons, and remove all the pith. Tip the fruit and pumpkin into a heavy-based pan with the sugar and vinegar. Bring to the boil over a medium heat, then reduce the heat and leave to simmer uncovered, stirring occasionally, for about 40 minutes.

3 Wash the jars thoroughly in hot soapy water, rinse, then dry in a low oven. Cool the chutney, then transfer to the sterilised jars and seal.

PER TBSP 51 kcals, protein 1g, carbs 13g, fat 1g, sat fat none, fibre 1g, sugar 11g, salt 0.02g

Fragrant mango & apple chutney

Homemade chutney makes a welcome gift for a friend. Cooking apples form a lovely pulpy base to the chutney while not overpowering the flavour of the mango.

**TAKES 2 HOURS ● MAKES ABOUT
4 × 450ML/16FL OZ JARS**

3 large ripe mangoes (about 1kg/2lb 4oz), peeled and stoned
2 tbsp sunflower oil
2 onions, halved and thinly sliced
thumb-size piece ginger, peeled and cut into thin shreds
10 green cardamom pods
1 cinnamon stick
½ tsp cumin seeds
½ tsp coriander seeds, lightly crushed
¼ tsp black onion seeds (nigella or kalonji)
½ tsp ground turmeric
2 Bramley apples (about 500g/1lb 2oz), peeled, cored and chopped
1 large red chilli, deseeded and finely chopped
375ml/13fl oz white wine vinegar
400g/14oz golden caster sugar
1 tsp salt

1 Cut the mango flesh into pieces and set aside. Heat the oil in a large, deep sauté pan, add the onions and fry for a few minutes until starting to soften. Stir in the ginger and cook, stirring frequently, for 8–10 minutes until the onion is golden. Stir in the spices, except the turmeric, and fry until toasted.

2 Stir in the turmeric, add the apples and pour in 450ml/16fl oz water, then cover the pan and cook for 10 minutes. Stir in the mango and chilli, cover, and cook for a further 20 minutes until the apple is pulpy and the mango is tender.

3 Pour in the vinegar and stir in the sugar and salt. Leave to simmer, uncovered, for 30 minutes, stirring frequently until the mixture is pulpy rather than watery. Meanwhile, thoroughly wash the jars, rinse, and dry in a low oven. Spoon the chutney into the sterilised jars.

PER TBSP 17 kcals, protein none, carbs 4g, fat none, sat fat none, fibre none, sugar 4g, salt none

Homemade tomato chutney

Whether you've grown your own or brought back some flavour-packed tomatoes from the market, this easy chutney is a good one to share with friends.

TAKES 1 HOUR 40 MINUTES
- **MAKES ABOUT 1KG /2LB 4OZ**

500g/1lb 2oz red onions, finely sliced
1kg/2lb 4oz tomatoes, chopped
4 garlic cloves, sliced
1 red chilli, chopped (optional)
4cm/1¾in piece ginger, peeled
   and chopped
250g/9oz brown sugar
150ml/¼ pint red wine vinegar
5 cardamom seeds
½ tsp paprika

1 Tip all the ingredients into a large heavy-based pan and bring to a gentle simmer, stirring frequently. Simmer for 1 hour, then bring to a gentle boil so that the mixture turns dark, jammy and shiny.

2 Thoroughly wash the jars in hot soapy water, rinse, and dry in a low oven. Spoon the chutney into the sterilised jars and allow to cool before covering. This chutney will keep for 6 weeks and is good with Cheddar and crusty bread.

PER TBSP 35 kcals, protein 1g, carbs 9g, fat none, sat fat none, fibre 1g, sugar 8g, salt 0.02g

Pear & dried apricot chutney

This is a great recipe for using up a glut of garden fruit. The fresh ginger adds a kick to the tempting combination of fruity flavours.

TAKES 2 HOURS ● **MAKES ABOUT 850ML/1½ PINTS**

425g/15oz ripe tomatoes, peeled, deseeded and chopped

425g/15oz caster sugar

140g/5oz cooking apples, peeled, cored and chopped

140g/5oz onions, finely chopped

140g/5oz dried apricots, chopped

3 tbsp chopped ginger

2 tsp salt

450ml/16fl oz white wine vinegar

1.25kg/2lb 12oz pears, peeled, cored and cut into bite-sized pieces

1 Combine all the ingredients, except the pears, in a large, heavy-based pan and bring to the boil. Simmer, uncovered, over a very low heat, stirring occasionally with a wooden spoon. Continue to cook for about 1 hour, giving the chutney a stir every 10 minutes, until the mixture is syrupy. Add the chopped pears and cook for another 30 minutes, stirring once in a while.

2 Wash the jars thoroughly in hot soapy water, rinse, then dry in a low oven. Leave the chutney to cool completely, then transfer to the sterilised jars.

PER TBSP 78 kcals, protein 1g, carbs 20g, fat 1g, sat fat none, fibre 1g, sugar 13g, salt 0.31g

Red onion marmalade

This is good with pâtés and terrines, but it's also great as part of a ploughman's lunch. Slow cooking is the secret of really soft and sticky onions – so don't rush that part.

TAKES 2–2¼ HOURS ● MAKES 4 × 450ML/16FL OZ JARS

140g/5oz butter
4 tbsp olive oil
2kg/4lb 8oz red onions, halved and thinly sliced
4 garlic cloves, thinly sliced
140g/5oz golden caster sugar
1 tbsp fresh thyme leaves
pinch of chilli flakes (optional)
75cl bottle red wine
350ml/12fl oz sherry vinegar or red wine vinegar
200ml/7fl oz port

1 Melt the butter with the oil in a large, heavy-based pan over a high heat. Tip in the onions and garlic, and stir so they are glossed with butter. Sprinkle over the sugar, thyme, chilli, if using, and some salt and pepper. Give everything a good stir and reduce the heat slightly. Cook, uncovered, for 40–50 minutes, stirring occasionally. The onions are ready when all their juices have evaporated and they're really soft and sticky.

2 Pour in the wine, vinegar and port, and simmer, still uncovered, over a high heat for 25–30 minutes, stirring every so often until the onions are a deep mahogany colour and the liquid has reduced by two-thirds.

3 Wash the jars thoroughly in hot soapy water, rinse, then dry in a low oven. Leave the onions to cool in the pan, then scoop them into the sterilised jars and seal. The marmalade can be eaten straight away, but it also keeps in the fridge for up to 3 months.

PER TBSP 40 kcals, protein 0.3g, carbs 4g, fat 2g, sat fat 1g, fibre 0.4g, sugar 4g, salt 0.03g

Quince jam

This is one of the easiest jams to make. Quinces are so high in pectin (the natural gelling agent that sets jam) that you just need to boil them up and sieve into jars.

TAKES ABOUT 2 HOURS • MAKES 850ML/1½ PINTS
1kg/2lb 4 oz quinces (about 4 fruits)
1kg/2lb 4 oz granulated sugar

1 You don't need to peel or core the fruit, simply chop the whole lot into chunks and tip it into a pan with the sugar. Add enough water to cover, bring to the boil, reduce the heat and simmer for 1½–1¾ hours, mashing the fruit after 45 minutes. Cook the jam until all the liquid has evaporated.

2 Wash the jars thoroughly in hot soapy water, rinse, then dry in a low oven.

3 Towards the end of the cooking time, stir the jam frequently to stop it burning on the bottom of the pan. Push the jam through a sieve into a bowl then spoon it into the sterilised jars. Good with a wedge of mature Cheddar or spread on buttered toast.

PER TBSP 123 kcals, protein 1g, carbs 33g, fat none, sat fat none, fibre none, sugar 31g, salt 0.01g

Spicy blackberry chutney

Blackberries have such a short season, so make this wonderful chutney while they're still around. When the season's over, you'll be glad you did.

TAKES 15 MINUTES • MAKES ABOUT 400ML/14FL OZ

500g/1lb 2oz blackberries
140g/5oz caster sugar
140g/5oz red onions, sliced
3 tbsp chopped ginger
2 tbsp Dijon mustard
150ml/¼ pint white wine vinegar

1 Combine all the ingredients, except the vinegar, in a large pan. Stir the mixture over a medium heat until the blackberries burst. Season with salt and pepper to taste. Add the vinegar and allow the mixture to simmer, uncovered, for 10 minutes.

2 Wash the jar thoroughly in hot soapy water, rinse, then dry in a low oven. Cool the chutney, transfer to a sterilised jar and seal immediately.

PER TBSP 50 kcals, protein 1g, carbs 12g, fat 1g, sat fat none, fibre 1g, sugar 9g, salt 0.15g

Rhubarb & ginger jam

Forced rhubarb has a delicate, sweet taste and a beautiful pink colour. This flavour combination is perfect with freshly baked scones and clotted cream.

TAKES 35 MINUTES, PLUS SOAKING
- **MAKES 4 × 450ML/16FL OZ JARS**

1kg/2lb 4oz pink rhubarb (trimmed weight), washed and sliced into 2cm/¾in pieces

1kg/2lb 4oz jam sugar

zest and juice 1 lemon

50g/2oz stem or crystallised ginger, finely chopped

4cm/1½in piece ginger, peeled

1 Tip the rhubarb into a large ceramic bowl and add the sugar, lemon zest and juice, and chopped ginger. Finely grate the peeled piece of ginger over the rhubarb. Stir, cover, and leave for 2 hours, stirring occasionally, to allow the sugar to dissolve.

2 Pop a few saucers in the freezer. Pour the rhubarb and the juices into a preserving pan, stir over a medium heat until the sugar has completely dissolved, then bring to the boil. Cook at a swift pace until the rhubarb is tender and the jam has reached setting point – roughly 10–15 minutes. Thoroughly wash the jars, rinse, then dry in a low oven.

3 To test for a set, drop ½ teaspoon jam on to a cold saucer, leave for 30 seconds, then gently push it with your finger. If the jam wrinkles, it is ready. If not, continue to cook for a couple of minutes and test again. Remove the pan from the heat, leave for 2–3 minutes and pour the jam into sterilised jars. Seal immediately.

PER ROUNDED TSP 55 kcals, protein none, carbs 15g, fat none, sat fat none, fibre none, sugar 15g, salt none

Speedy summer fruits jam

Cleverly, this tempting jam is made entirely in the microwave in just 20 minutes – with no tricky tests for setting point. A delicious way to enjoy summer all year round.

TAKES 20 MINUTES • MAKES 4 SMALL JARS

500g/1lb 2oz mixed summer berries (raspberries, strawberries, blackcurrants, etc)
500g/1lb 2oz jam sugar

1 Wash the jars thoroughly in hot soapy water, rinse, then dry in a low oven.
2 Briefly blend the fruit and put in a large microwave-proof bowl with the sugar. Microwave on High for 3 minutes, then stir well. Microwave for a further 3 minutes on High, stirring often. Finish with a further 2 minutes.
3 Pour the jam into the warm sterilised jars. Once bottled and cool, the jam is ready to eat. It will keep in a cool, dark place for up to 6 months. Keep in the fridge once opened.

PER SERVING 70 kcals, protein none, carbs 19g, fat none, sat fat none, fibre none, sugar 19g, salt none

Low-sugar marmalade

This marmalade is lower in sugar than traditional recipes but the flavour is just as intense. You can store it, unopened, for up to 3 months in a cool place.

TAKES 1¾ HOURS ● MAKES ABOUT 2.25KG/5LB

900g/2lb Seville oranges
600ml/1 pint pure unsweetened apple juice
900g/2lb jam sugar

1 Cut the oranges into thin slices. Remove the pips and tie them in a muslin bag. Put the orange slices in a preserving pan with the apple juice and the pips. Bring to the boil then simmer very gently for 30–40 minutes, or until the orange peel can be pierced easily with a fork. The mixture will be very thick, with little liquid.

2 Add the jam sugar and stir over a low heat until it has completely dissolved, about 5 minutes. Bring to a good rolling boil then bubble for 4 minutes. Take the pan off the heat and skim any scum from the surface.

3 Wash your jars thoroughly in hot soapy water, rinse, then dry in a low oven. Remove the muslin bag and leave the marmalade to stand in the pan for 15 minutes to cool a little, and to allow the peel to settle. Spoon into sterilised jars, seal and label.

PER TBSP 44 kcals, protein 0.1g, carbs 12g, fat none, sat fat none, fibre 0.2g, sugar 12g, salt 0.31g

Apricot conserve

Cutting down on the sugar to make this conserve means you get the full flavour of the fresh apricots without it being oversweet. Store in the fridge for 4–6 weeks.

TAKES 55 MINUTES • **MAKES ABOUT 3 × 450ML/16FL OZ JARS**

1.5kg/3lb 5oz apricots, halved and stoned (reserve stones)
200ml/7fl oz apple juice
1kg/2lb 4oz preserving sugar
juice 1 large lemon
knob of butter

1 Put two small plates in the freezer. Chop the apricots and put them in a large pan with the apple juice. Crack some of the kernels to extract the nut inside, and add them to the pan to give extra flavour. Bring to the boil, reduce the heat and simmer for 10 minutes, until the apricots are softened.

2 Stir in the sugar and lemon juice, then stir well over a moderate heat to dissolve the sugar. Increase the heat and boil for 20 minutes until the jam has set. Test by spooning a little jam on to a cold plate. After a moment, push the jam with your finger; if it wrinkles, it is ready. If not, return to the boil for 5 minutes then test again.

3 Wash the jars thoroughly in hot soapy water, rinse, then dry in a low oven to sterilise them.

4 Remove the jam from the heat, then stir in the butter to remove any scum. Cool for 10 minutes, stir, then ladle into warm sterilised jars.

PER TBSP 57 kcals, protein none, carbs 15g, fat none, sat fat none, fibre none, sugar 15g, salt none

Really fruity strawberry jam

This is a soft-set jam with juicy strawberry chunks. Don't be tempted to make it in larger batches: you'd have to cook it for longer and the flavour won't be as fresh.

TAKES 25 MINUTES, PLUS STANDING
- **MAKES 3 × 450ML/16FL OZ JARS**

1.25kg/2lb 12oz firm ripe strawberries, washed, hulled and large ones halved
1kg pack jam sugar
juice 1 lemon
knob of unsalted butter

1 Layer the strawberries and sugar in a large bowl, finishing with a layer of sugar. Cover the bowl and leave for 24 hours. Put a couple of saucers in the freezer.

2 By the next day the juices will have been drawn out from the fruit, giving you a bowl of berries in a sugary pink syrup. If this hasn't happened, stir the berries then leave them for a few more hours.

3 Tip the mixture into a preserving pan over a low heat and warm to dissolve any remaining sugar. Bring to the boil, stirring frequently, until bubbling.

4 Pour in the lemon juice, return to the boil, then boil hard for 10 minutes, stirring occasionally. Add the butter to remove any scum. Remove the pan from the heat then drop a little jam on to one of the chilled saucers. Let it cool a little then push your finger through the jam; if it wrinkles, it is ready. Allow to cool for 30 minutes. Meanwhile, wash some jars in hot soapy water, rinse, then dry in a low oven. Spoon the jam into the jars.

PER TBSP 71 kcals, protein none, carbs 19g, fat none, sat fat none, fibre none, sugar 19g, salt 0.01g

Shortcut Seville marmalade

The Seville orange season is short, so make the most of it. This recipe saves hours on the traditional overnight method and the result is just as good.

**TAKES 2½ HOURS • MAKES ABOUT
4 × 450ML/16FL OZ JARS**
500g/1lb 2oz Seville oranges
1.5kg/3lb 5oz jam sugar

1 Put a saucer in the freezer. In a large pan, boil the whole oranges in 2 litres/3½ pints water until they are very soft – this will take about 2 hours. Using a slotted spoon, scoop out the oranges and set aside. Pour the liquid into a preserving pan or any large pan.
2 When cool enough to handle, cut the oranges into wedges, remove the pips then gently squeeze the wedges over the pan, as they'll be very juicy. Very thinly slice the oranges, then add them to the pan with the jam sugar. Dissolve the sugar over a medium heat then boil for 7–10 minutes, stirring occasionally, until a little of the mixture dropped on to the chilled saucer sets and wrinkles when you push your finger through it.
3 Wash the jars thoroughly in hot soapy water, rinse, then dry in a low oven. When the marmalade is ready, leave it to settle for 15 minutes before potting it into the sterilised jars.

PER TBSP 75 kcals, protein 0.1g, carbs 20g, fat none, sat fat none, fibre 0.2g, sugar 20g, salt 0.31g

Balsamic pickled shallots

These shallots make an impressive gift but are so easy to put together (once you've done the peeling) that even a first-time preserver could do it.

TAKES 1½ HOURS, PLUS 3 DAYS STANDING • MAKES 4 × 450ML/ 16FL OZ JARS

1.5kg/3lb 5oz small shallots or pearl onions
1 litre/1¾ pints white wine vinegar
150ml/¼ pint olive oil
600ml/1 pint water
140g/5oz golden caster sugar
1 tbsp salt
1 tsp black peppercorns, cracked
2 handfuls basil leaves
100ml/3½fl oz balsamic vinegar

1 Tip the shallots or onions into a large bowl, pour over a kettleful of boiling water, leave to stand for a minute, then drain. When cool enough to handle, sit down, turn the radio on and get peeling.

2 Wash the jars well in soapy water, rinse, then dry in a low oven. Set the peeled shallots or onions aside and place all the other ingredients except the balsamic vinegar into a large pan. Bring to the boil, lower the heat, then simmer for 3 minutes. Drop the shallots into the pan and simmer for around 8-10 minutes until just tender.

3 Use a slotted spoon to scoop out the shallots or onions and basil, and transfer them to the sterilised jars. Boil the liquid vigorously for 5 minutes, turn the heat off, stir in the balsamic vinegar, then pour over the shallots to cover. Seal the jars and leave for at least 3 days. Will keep for up to 3 months.

PER SERVING 25 kcals, protein 1g, carbs 3g, fat 1g, sat fat none, fibre 1g, sugar 3g, salt 0.26g

Slow-cooked tomatoes with basil

Just like their sun-dried and SunBlush cousins, these add a delicious, intense tomato flavour wherever they're used.

**TAKES 3–4 HOURS ● MAKES 3 ×
450ML/16FL OZ JARS**

3kg/6lb 8oz small tomatoes from the
    vine, halved
4 tsp herbes de Provence
500ml bottle light olive oil, plus extra
    for drizzling
large bunch basil, leaves only
2 tsp black peppercorns

1 Heat oven to 140C/120C fan/gas 1. Spread the tomato halves over two large baking sheets, cut-side up. Season with salt and pepper, scatter with the herbes de Provence and drizzle with a little olive oil. Roast in the oven for about 3–4 hours, or until semi-dried and intensely red. They should be dry in the middle and have a chewy texture – the best way to test is to try one.

2 Put a small basil leaf or piece of torn basil on top of each tomato half for the final hour of cooking. (The cooking time will vary depending on the juiciness of your tomatoes.) Wash the jars thoroughly in hot soapy water, rinse, then dry in a low oven.

3 Heat the oil and peppercorns in a pan. Pack the tomatoes into the sterilised jars and cover with the warm oil. Keep in the fridge for up to 1 week.

PER JAR 411 kcals, protein 7g, carbs 34g, fat 28g, sat fat 4g, fibre 10g, sugar 31g, salt 0.23g

Chestnuts in spiced syrup

These make an unusual and welcome gift. They are great for a last-minute dessert served with ice cream and they will keep unopened for several months in a cool place.

**TAKES 45 MINUTES ● MAKES 2 ×
375ML/13FL OZ JARS**

400g/14oz golden caster sugar
2 cinnamon sticks
4 star anise
8 whole cloves
1 tbsp whole allspice or coriander
  seeds
400g/14oz peeled whole canned or
  vacuum-packed chestnuts

1 Warm the sugar and 700ml/1¼ pints water in a large, shallow pan over a low heat until the sugar dissolves – do not let it boil or the syrup will be cloudy. Add the spices, bring to the boil and simmer for 15–20 minutes.

2 Add the chestnuts to the syrup, cover and continue infusing over a very low heat for 10 minutes – make sure the syrup doesn't boil, or the chestnuts will break up. Leave to cool for 5 minutes.

3 Meanwhile, wash the jars thoroughly in hot soapy water, rinse, and dry in a low oven. Transfer the chestnuts to the warm, sterilised jars using a slotted spoon. Divide the spices evenly among the jars. Ladle the syrup over the chestnuts, covering them completely. Seal with a tight-fitting lid.

PER JAR (WITH SYRUP) 1,145 kcals, protein 5g, carbs 286g, fat 6g, sat fat 1g, fibre 8g, sugar 224g, salt 0.09g

Homemade ketchup

When tomatoes are in season and plentiful, it's really worth making your own delicious ketchup. Add some tomato purée for thickness and colour.

TAKES 1 HOUR 20 MINUTES
- **MAKES ABOUT 2 LITRES/3½ PINTS**

4 good-size onions, very roughly chopped
250g/9oz celery, very roughly chopped
5 tbsp vegetable or olive oil
4 garlic cloves, sliced
1 tsp ground coriander
1 short cinnamon stick
1 tsp ground allspice
½ tsp ground black pepper
2 tsp celery salt
2kg/4lb 8oz ripe tomatoes, roughly chopped
3 tbsp tomato purée
½ tsp Tabasco
200ml/7fl oz white wine vinegar
200g/7oz golden caster sugar

1 Put the onions and celery into a food processor and whizz until finely chopped. Heat the oil in a very large pan, add the onions and celery, cover, then soften over a low heat for around 5 minutes. Add the garlic, cook for 5 minutes more, then tip in the spices and cook for 1 minute.

2 Now stir in all the remaining ingredients and bring to the boil. Keep on a bubbling simmer, uncovered, for 1 hour until the tomatoes are squashy and the liquid has reduced by several centimetres.

3 Whizz the mix with a stick blender until smooth, then sieve into a bowl. The ketchup will thicken a little when it cools, but if yours seems very runny (this will depend on the juiciness of the tomatoes), put it back on the heat and cook it a little longer, stirring often, until reduced. Keep the ketchup in an airtight container in the fridge for 3 months, or freeze in batches.

PER TBSP 25 kcals, protein none, carbs 4g, fat 1g, sat fat none, fibre none, sugar 4g, salt 0.08g

Cranberry oatcakes

Dried cranberries give these easy, crunchy oatcakes a modern twist. The hint of fruit works well with a slice of creamy Stilton.

TAKES 35 MINUTES ● MAKES ABOUT 20 SMALL OATCAKES

225g/8oz medium oatmeal, plus extra for dusting
¼ tsp bicarbonate of soda
¼ tsp salt
25g/1oz dried sweetened cranberries, roughly chopped
1 tbsp unsalted butter

1 Heat oven to 180C/160C fan/gas 4. Mix the oatmeal, bicarbonate of soda and salt in a bowl. Stir in the cranberries. Heat the butter and 150ml/¼ pint water in a pan until the butter melts.

2 Make a well in the centre of the oatmeal mix, pour in the liquid and use a palette knife to mix everything together. The mixture will seem a bit wet, but the oatmeal will gradually absorb all the liquid to give a soft dough.

3 Lightly dust a work surface with oatmeal. Tip out the dough, then roll out to about 5mm thick. Use a small cutter to stamp out oatcakes. Re-roll and re-use any trimmings.

4 Brush off any excess oatmeal, then space out the oatcakes over two baking sheets. Bake for about 20 minutes, carefully turning every 5 minutes to stop them steaming and going stodgy. When cooked, they should be crisp and lightly golden. Cool on a wire rack.

PER OATCAKE 54 kcals, protein 1g, carbs 9g, fat 2g, sat fat 1g, fibre 1g, sugar 1g, salt 0.12g

Aubergines & feta with chilli

These Greek-style aubergines are delicious served with triangles of toasted pitta bread, houmous and fresh mint. Keep in the fridge for up to 1 week.

TAKES 1 HOUR, PLUS OVERNIGHT SALTING ● MAKES 3 × 450ML/16FL OZ JARS

8 large aubergines
500g box sea salt flakes (you won't need the whole box)
200ml/7fl oz red wine vinegar
500ml bottle light olive oil
3 tsp dried oregano
1 tsp chilli flakes
2 tsp black peppercorns
200g pack feta cheese, drained and cubed

1 Thinly slice the aubergines lengthways. Layer the slices in a colander, sprinkle generously with salt and cover with cling film. Sit the colander over a large bowl and leave in the fridge overnight.

2 Discard the juice from the aubergines. Put the vinegar into a large pan with an equal quantity of water and bring to the boil. Add the aubergine slices, return to the boil, turn down and simmer for 3 minutes. Dry on kitchen paper. (You may need to do this in batches.)

3 Heat a griddle pan until hot but not smoking. Brush the aubergine slices with a little oil on both sides and cook for 2 minutes each side until well charred. Wash the jars thoroughly in hot soapy water, rinse, then dry in a low oven.

4 Heat the remaining oil with the oregano, chilli and peppercorns in a pan over a low heat until warm but not too hot. Pack the aubergines into jars with the cheese cubes, top up with the herby oil and seal.

PER JAR 548 kcals, protein 19g, carbs 24g, fat 42g, sat fat 12g, fibre 18g, sugar 20g, salt 3.50g

Gooseberry & elderflower curd

If you want a chunkier curd, don't sieve the gooseberries, but you will need to top and tail them before cooking.

TAKES 40 MINUTES, PLUS CHILLING
- **MAKES 750ML/1¼ PINTS**

500g/1lb 2oz gooseberries
250g/9oz golden caster sugar
85g/3oz cold butter, cut into pieces
3 eggs, beaten
3 tbsp elderflower cordial

1 Tip the gooseberries into a pan with a splash of water, cover, place on a high heat and cook for 5 minutes until the gooseberries have stewed down to a pulp. Push the gooseberries and juice through a sieve into a large bowl.

2 Tip all the other ingredients into the bowl with the gooseberry purée and place the bowl over a pan of gently simmering water. Stirring constantly, cook everything for about 20 minutes until you have a smooth curd about the thickness of custard.

3 Wash the jars thoroughly in hot soapy water, rinse, then dry in a low oven.

4 Pour the curd into the sterilised jars and cover with a disc of greaseproof paper. The curd will need to chill for at least 3 hours before it's spreadable. Delicious on toast or spread on to shortbread. This will keep for up to 6 weeks, but once opened should be used within 2 days.

PER SERVING 70 kcals, protein 1g, carbs 10g, fat 3g, sat fat 2g, fibre none, sugar 10g, salt 0.07g

Chargrilled artichokes with lemon

All artichoke recipes call for a good dousing in lemon juice as it stops the cut heads discolouring. Keep in the fridge for up to 1 week.

TAKES 1 HOUR 20 MINUTES • MAKES 2 × 450ML/16FL OZ JARS

juice and zest 1 unwaxed lemon
20 baby globe artichokes
250ml/9fl oz white wine vinegar
2 tbsp light olive oil
500ml bottle light olive oil
2 tsp mixed peppercorns

1 Pour the lemon juice into a bowl of cold water. Cut off the outer leaves of the artichokes until you reach greenish-yellow leaves. Trim the stalks to 5cm, then quarter the heads. Rub the cut sides with a squeezed lemon half and put in the lemony water.

2 Bring some water to the boil in a large pan. Add 100ml/3½fl oz of the vinegar and the artichokes. Simmer for 15–18 minutes. Drain and tip into a bowl, toss with the 2 tablespoons of oil and season.

3 Griddle the artichoke quarters on a hot griddle pan until golden and charred at the edges. Wash the jars thoroughly in hot soapy water, rinse, and dry in a low oven.

4 In another pan, warm the olive oil, zest and peppercorns until the zest starts to sizzle. Fish out the zest with a slotted spoon. Warm the remaining vinegar in a pan until almost boiling.

5 Pack the artichokes and zest into jars, pour over the warmed vinegar, then top up with warm oil to cover. Seal while warm, then allow to cool.

PER JAR 404 kcals, protein 3g, carbs 14g, fat 38g, sat fat 5g, fibre 5g, sugar 1g, salt 2.74g

Smoky paprika peppers

These peppers are great to nibble on their own, or delicious stirred into pasta or sprinkled on top of a pizza. Keep in the fridge for up to 1 week.

**TAKES 40 MINUTES • MAKES 3 ×
450ML/16FL OZ JARS**
500ml bottle mild olive oil
2 tsp sweet smoked paprika
1 garlic clove, thinly sliced
1 tbsp black peppercorns
1 tbsp fennel seeds
8 red peppers, halved and deseeded
8 yellow peppers, halved and deseeded
300ml/½ pint white wine vinegar
small bunch flat-leaf parsley, chopped

1 Gently heat the oil in a pan with the paprika and garlic for 5 minutes, then cool. Lay a piece of muslin over a sieve and strain the liquid into a bowl, discarding the garlic and paprika, to leave bright orange, scented oil. In another pan, dry-fry the spices for 1 minute to release their aromas. Add to the paprika oil and set aside.

2 Heat grill to high. Grill the pepper halves on two baking sheets, skin-side up, for 15 minutes until the skins are blackened. Transfer the peppers to plastic food bags, seal and leave to cool. Once cool enough to handle, slip off the skins and tear the flesh into large pieces.

3 Wash the jars thoroughly, rinse, then dry in a low oven. Bring the vinegar and 300ml/½ pint water to a simmer in a large pan and tip in the peppers. Bring back to a simmer for 3 minutes, drain well and pack into jars. Gently reheat the spiced oil for a few minutes, then pour over the peppers, stir in some chopped parsley and seal.

PER JAR 464 kcals, protein 9g, carbs 46g, fat 28g, sat fat 4g, fibre 12g, sugar 42g, salt 0.09g

Fig & walnut slice

Paired with a favourite cheese or two and maybe a bottle of port, this figgy treat is a great idea for a cheese-lover.

TAKES 15 MINUTES • SERVES 12

50g/2oz whole almonds, toasted
250g/9oz dried figs, hard stalk
    removed, chopped
50g/2oz dried apricots, halved
50g/2oz walnuts, halved
½ tbsp brandy
½ tbsp clear honey
pinch ground cloves

1 Pulse the almonds in a food processor until most are finely chopped. Remove and transfer to a bowl. Whizz the figs until they form a sticky paste then add this to the almonds with the remaining ingredients. Mix well, then form into a sausage shape and allow to dry, uncovered, in the fridge or a cool, dry place for a week.

2 Wrap and tie it in baking parchment if you are giving it away, or slice and serve it alongside your favourite cheeses. Will keep in a cool place for up to 2 months.

PER SERVING 113 kcals, protein 2g, carbs 14g, fat 6g, sat fat 1g, fibre 2g, sugar 14g, salt 0.04g

Cherry & cinnamon conserve

Cherries are low in pectin so it's essential to use jam sugar with added pectin to help this conserve to set. Boiling for just a short time helps retain the wonderful flavour.

TAKES 55 MINUTES • MAKES ABOUT 1KG/2LB 4OZ

1kg/2lb 4oz cherries, stoned
1 cinnamon stick
zest and juice 2 lemons
500g/1lb 2oz jam sugar

1 Put a couple of saucers into the freezer. Roughly chop about a third of the cherries. Put all the cherries into a large pan with the cinnamon stick, broken in half, the lemon zest and juice and 150ml/¼ pint water. Bring the fruit gently to the boil, then reduce the heat and simmer for 20 minutes, stirring occasionally, until the cherries are softened.

2 Add the sugar, stir until dissolved, then increase the heat and boil hard for 4–5 minutes until the conserve is softly set. To test this, take a saucer from the freezer and spoon a little jam on to it. Push your finger through the jam – if it wrinkles on the surface it is ready, if not, reboil for a few minutes more, then test again. Wash the jars in hot soapy water, rinse, then dry in a low oven. Spoon the jam into the warm, sterilised jars, seal, and label. Once open, keep in the fridge.

PER TBSP 36 kcals, protein none, carbs 9g, fat none, sat fat none, fibre none, sugar 9g, salt none

Sweet chilli jam

If you're making this for someone who likes things really spicy, just swap a few of the red chillies for fiery little bird's-eye or Scotch bonnet varieties.

TAKES 1 HOUR 20 MINUTES • MAKES 4 SMALL JARS

8 red peppers, deseeded and roughly chopped

10 red chillies, roughly chopped (with seeds)

finger-size piece ginger, peeled and roughly chopped

8 garlic cloves, peeled

400g can cherry tomatoes

750g/1lb 10oz golden caster sugar

250ml/9fl oz red wine vinegar

1 Tip the peppers, chillies, ginger and garlic into a food processor, then whizz until very finely chopped. Scrape into a heavy-based pan with the tomatoes, sugar and vinegar, then bring everything to the boil. Skim off any scum that comes to the surface, then turn the heat down to a simmer and cook for about 50 minutes, stirring occasionally.

2 Wash the jars in hot soapy water, rinse, then dry in a low oven.

3 Once the jam is becoming sticky, continue cooking for 10–15 minutes more, stirring frequently so that it doesn't catch and burn. It should now look like thick, bubbling lava. Cool slightly, transfer to the sterilised jars, then leave to cool completely. Keeps for 3 months in a cool, dark cupboard. Refrigerate once opened.

PER JAR 857 kcals, protein 5g, carbs 220g, fat 1g, sat fat none, fibre 6g, sugar 218g, salt 0.34g

Grape jelly

Adding lemon juice here counterbalances the sweetness of the grapes. This makes an unusual treat for a friend and will keep unopened for up to 3 months.

TAKES 30 MINUTES, PLUS STRAINING
- **MAKES 600ML/1 PINT**

1kg/2lb 4oz red grapes, preferably with seeds (stripped from the stalks)
450g/1lb jam sugar
juice 1 lemon

1 Tip the grapes into a large pan set over a low heat. Cover and cook gently for 5 minutes until the juices start to run. Using a potato masher, mash up the grapes. Leave to cook for 10 minutes, mashing occasionally until the grapes are falling apart. Place a clean tea towel in a sieve set over a bowl, then pour the grape mixture into this. Let the mixture drip through for at least 1 hour or preferably overnight.

2 Thoroughly wash the jars, rinse, and dry in a low oven. Measure out the collected juice (you should have about 600ml/1 pint) and pour it into a pan with the sugar and lemon juice. Set the pan over a high heat and bring to the boil; let the mixture bubble until it reaches 105C,220F on a sugar thermometer, or put a saucer in the freezer for 5 minutes then pour a little juice on to the chilled saucer. After 1 minute, run your finger through; if the jam wrinkles, it's ready. Pour the hot jam into the jars.

PER SERVING 57 kcals, protein none, carbs 15g, fat none, sat fat none, fibre none, sugar 15g, salt none

Plumbrillo

Quince paste or membrillo is traditionally served with cheese, but quinces can be hard to get hold of. This plum version is intensely fruity and makes a good alternative.

TAKES 1 HOUR 40 MINUTES • MAKES ABOUT 7 X 100ML/3½FL OZ POTS

2kg/4lb 8oz black or red plums, stoned and quartered
1kg bag jam sugar

1 Put the plums into a preserving pan. Add 500ml/18fl oz cold water and bring to a boil. Cover and simmer for about 45 minutes until completely cooked down, pulpy and dark, dark red.

2 Sieve the fruit and juice through a nylon sieve back into the pan – make sure you get every bit of pulp out of the mix that you can. Wash the jars in hot soapy water, rinse, then dry in a low oven.

3 Stir the sugar into the fruit, then stir over a low heat until dissolved. Now turn up the heat and bubble for 25 minutes or until you have a thick, dark and fruity purée. Keep stirring so that the bottom doesn't catch – it's ready when the spoon leaves a trail along the bottom of pan for a split second before the paste floods back into the gap. Pot the hot mix into small jars, seal, then leave to set. Will keep for up to 6 months.

PER SERVING 56 kcals, protein none, carbs 15g, fat none, sat fat none, fibre none, sugar 15g, salt none

Spiced arancello

Boozy, spiced and sweet, this liqueur is based on the classic Italian drink arancello. It is superb served straight, or will give an exquisite orangey kick to puds and ice cream.

TAKES 1¼ HOURS, PLUS 2 WEEKS STANDING • MAKES ABOUT 2.5 LITRES/4½ PINTS

5 large oranges
1 cinnamon stick
2–3 cardamom pods
1 vanilla pod
1-litre bottle vodka
600g/1lb 5oz caster sugar
a few extra oranges, cinnamon sticks, cardamom and vanilla pods, to decorate

1 Pare the zest from the oranges using a peeler, making sure that none of the bitter white pith is left on the peel. Put the zest, spices and vanilla pod in one large or several smaller clean jars, then tip in the vodka. Seal and leave for a week, shaking the jar each day.

2 After a week, you're ready for the next stage. Boil a kettle of water. Put the sugar in a heatproof bowl, then pour over 500ml/18fl oz boiling water, stirring until the sugar dissolves. Add to the vodka mix, then leave for another week, shaking the jar regularly. Strain into decorative bottles, discarding the peel and spices, and store in a cool place. Before giving the arancello as a present, drop some fresh spices and zest into each bottle to decorate. Will keep bottled for 6 months.

PER SERVING (85ml/3fl oz) 179 kcals, protein none, carbs 27g, fat none, sat fat none, fibre none, sugar 27g, salt none

Homemade elderflower cordial

The secret to making a well-flavoured elderflower cordial is to pick the flowers on a sunny day before it gets too hot, then use them as soon as possible.

TAKES 30 MINUTES, PLUS STEEPING

● **MAKES ABOUT 4 LITRES/ 7 PINTS**

2.5kg/5lb 8oz white sugar, either granulated or caster

1.5 litres/2¾ pints water

2 unwaxed lemons

20 fresh elderflower heads, stalks trimmed

85g/3oz citric acid (from chemists or home stores)

1 Put the sugar and water into the largest saucepan you have. Gently heat, without boiling, until the sugar has dissolved. Give it an occasional stir. Pare the zest from the lemons, then slice the lemons into rounds.

2 Once the sugar has dissolved, bring the syrup to the boil, then turn off the heat. Fill a large bowl with cold water. Give the flowers a gentle swish around to loosen any dirt or bugs. Lift out the flowers, shake and transfer to the syrup along with the lemon rounds, zest and citric acid, then stir well. Cover the pan and leave to infuse for 24 hours.

3 Line a colander with a clean tea towel, then sit it over a large bowl. Ladle in the syrup – let it drip slowly through. Discard any bits left in the towel. Use a funnel and a ladle to fill sterilised bottles (wash glass bottles well with hot soapy water, rinse, then leave to dry in a low oven). The cordial is ready to drink straight away and will keep in the fridge for up to 6 weeks.

PER 250ML/9FL OZ 619 kcals, protein none, carbs 165g, fat none, sat fat none, fibre none, sugar 165g, salt 0.03g

Chocolate–peppermint snaps

These easy-to-make chocs are perfect with an after-dinner coffee, so pack them into a pretty box to take to a friend or to a dinner party.

TAKES 5 MINUTES, PLUS CHILLING
• **SERVES 8**

300g/10oz dark chocolate
3 tbsp demerara sugar
½ tsp peppermint essence

1 Melt the dark chocolate in a heatproof bowl set over a pan of barely simmering water. Line a large baking sheet with baking parchment.

2 Mix the demerara sugar with the peppermint essence. When the chocolate has melted, cool for 1–2 minutes. (If the chocolate is too hot when it's mixed with the sugar, the sugar will melt and you'll lose your crunch, so don't be too hasty.) Mix the peppermint sugar into the chocolate, then pour on to the baking sheet. Spread to a very thin layer and chill until completely firm. Snap into shards to serve.

PER SERVING 214 kcals, protein 2g, carbs 30g, fat 11g, sat fat 6g, fibre 1g, sugar 30g, salt 0.01g

Melting middle truffles

These are the perfect not-too-dark truffles for a milk chocolate lover. You'll get messy making them, but that's all part of the fun.

TAKES 50 MINUTES, PLUS FREEZING
- **MAKES 40**

½ × 450g jar dulce de leche caramel toffee
100g/4oz dark chocolate (70% cocoa solids), chopped
2 × 200g bars milk chocolate, chopped
142ml pot double cream
1 tsp vanilla extract
about 85g/3oz cocoa powder, to coat

1 Heat the dulce de leche in a pan for 1 minute until runny, then stir in the dark chocolate and leave to melt. Stir until smooth. Cover a dinner plate with cling film, oil the cling film well, then tip the mix on to it. Cool, then freeze for 2 hours until very firm.

2 Put the milk chocolate into a bowl. Bring the cream to the boil in another pan, then pour it over the chocolate. Leave for 2 minutes, then add the vanilla and stir until smooth. Cool, then chill until set.

3 Peel the caramel from the cling film, then snip it into thumbnail-size pieces: wet kitchen scissors work best. Spread the cocoa over a large baking sheet. Take a heaped teaspoon of truffle mix then, with cocoa-dusted hands, poke in a caramel chunk. Squash the truffle mix around the caramel to seal, then roll into a ball. Put on to the baking sheet and shake to coat in cocoa. Repeat with the rest of mix. Chill until needed.

PER TRUFFLE 112 kcals, protein 1g, carbs 12g, fat 7g, sat fat 4g, fibre 1g, sugar 10g, salt 0.05g

Chocolate fudge

The boiling fudge gets very hot, so it's best not to let children help with the first part of this recipe. Let them get stuck in with the decorating though!

TAKES 25 MINUTES, PLUS COOLING
● **MAKES 30–36 SQUARES**
397g can condensed milk
150ml/¼ pint milk
450g/1lb demerara sugar
100g/4oz butter
1 tbsp liquid glucose
100g/4oz dark chocolate, melted

TO DECORATE
50g/2oz white chocolate, melted

1 Line an 18cm-square baking tin with baking parchment. Gently heat all the ingredients, except the chocolates, in a large non-stick pan, stirring until all the sugar dissolves.

2 Bring to the boil and simmer gently for about 15 minutes, stirring frequently with a wooden spoon. The mixture will thicken, so stir and scrape the pan or it can catch on the bottom and you will get burnt bits in the fudge. Remove the pan from the heat and cool for 5 minutes.

3 Stir in the melted dark chocolate, then beat the fudge until thick and grainy, about 5 minutes – this is easiest with a pair of electric beaters. Spread into the prepared tin and leave to cool. Once completely cold, cut the fudge into squares, then drizzle with melted white chocolate to decorate. Store in an airtight container for up to 1 week.

PER SERVING 130 kcals, protein 1g, carbs 22g, fat 5g, sat fat 3g, fibre none, sugar 22g, salt 0.09g

Blackcurrant jelly pastilles

If you haven't made jellies before because you find gelatine a bit fiddly, try these. They're made with pectin, a natural setting agent normally used in jam-making.

TAKES 35 MINUTES, PLUS CHILLING
- **MAKES ABOUT 49**

4 × 290g cans blackcurrants, drained
4 tsp lemon juice
450g/1lb golden caster sugar
4 tbsp liquid glucose
4 tbsp liquid pectin
about 100g/4oz granulated sugar,
    for rolling

1 Grease and line two 18cm-square baking tins with greaseproof paper. Put the blackcurrants into a food processor, then liquidise to a thick purée. Pour into a medium non-stick pan. Add the lemon juice, caster sugar, glucose and pectin, and gently heat the mixture, stirring until the sugar dissolves. Bring to the boil and keep boiling for 10 minutes, stirring until the mixture reduces by half and thickens. Remove from the heat, then spread into tins and leave to set to a thick jelly. Chill overnight or for at least 3 hours.

2 Tip the granulated sugar on to a tray. Lift the jelly out of the tins, keeping the lining paper attached. Cut each sheet into seven strips, then across to make 49 pastilles. Roll each pastille in granulated sugar until it coats all the sides, then drop one or two jellies into petit four cases. Sugar your hands if they get sticky. Store in an airtight container in the fridge for up to 1 week.

PER SERVING 55 kcals, protein none, carbs 15g, fat none, sat fat none, fibre none, sugar 14g, salt 0.01g

Chocolate-biscuit truffles

These crunchy, fruity truffles are really easy to make. Ring the changes by adding your own favourite dried fruits.

TAKES 25 MINUTES, PLUS CHILLING

● **MAKES ABOUT 30**

142ml pot double cream

150g bar white chocolate, broken into cubes

150g bar dark chocolate, broken into cubes

50g/2oz unsalted butter

4 shortbread fingers or biscuits, roughly crumbled

85g/3oz dried fruits (chopped apricots and cranberries are good)

zest 1 orange

icing sugar and cocoa powder, for rolling

1 Put the cream in a small pan and bring just to the boil. Put the chocolates in separate bowls, then divide the butter between each. Pour half the cream into each bowl of chocolate. Leave for about 1 minute then stir until melted and smooth. Allow to cool.

2 Divide the shortbread, fruit and orange zest between the bowls, stir, then chill for at least 4 hours until firm.

3 Using a teaspoon, scoop out the mixtures and form into small truffles. Sift the icing sugar on to a plate and roll the white chocolate truffles in it. Do the same with the cocoa and the dark chocolate truffles, then chill until set. These can be made up to a day ahead.

PER TRUFFLE 118 kcals, protein 1g, carbs 12g, fat 8g, sat fat 5g, fibre 1g, sugar 10g, salt 0.04 g

Bramble marshmallows

These fruity marshmallows are a gorgeous colour and taste wonderful. They take a bit of time and effort but they are certainly worth it. Best eaten on the day they are made.

TAKES 1 HOUR 10 MINUTES
● **MAKES ABOUT 50**

50g/2oz icing sugar
50g/2oz cornflour
9 sheets gelatine
450g/1lb granulated sugar
1 tbsp liquid glucose (find it in the
    baking aisle)
2 egg whites
1 tsp vanilla extract
140g/5oz blackberries

1 In a bowl, mix the icing sugar with the cornflour and set aside. Dissolve the gelatine in 150ml/¼ pint hot water in a heatproof jug. Line a 20 × 30cm tin with baking parchment and dust with some of the icing-sugar mix. Over a low heat, cook the granulated sugar, glucose and 200ml/7fl oz water in a heavy-based pan until the sugar has dissolved. Turn up the heat and boil until the mixture reaches firm ball stage on a sugar thermometer (125C/256F). Meanwhile, whisk the egg whites until stiff. When the syrup reaches the right stage, carefully pour it into a jug with the gelatine (it will be hot).
2 Continue whisking the whites while pouring in the syrup in a steady stream, then add the vanilla – the mixture will become shiny and thicken. Continue whisking for 10 minutes until very stiff. Pour half the mixture into the tin and scatter over the berries. Top with the remaining mixture and leave to set.
3 Cut the marshmallows into squares, and roll in the icing-sugar mix to coat.

PER SERVING 46 kcals, protein none, carbs 12g, fat none, sat fat none, fibre none, sugar 11g, salt 0.01g

White chocolate chip fudge

You can wrap the whole block of fudge in Cellophane, or cut it into squares and then box or bag it up. Use milk or dark chocolate chips, if you like.

TAKES 25 MINUTES, PLUS OVERNIGHT SETTING • MAKES 12 SQUARES

500g/1lb 2oz golden caster sugar
450ml/16fl oz double cream
3 tbsp liquid glucose
140g/5oz white chocolate, cut into chunks (not too small or they'll melt completely)

1 Line a 22cm-square non-stick tin with baking parchment. Put the sugar, cream and glucose in a pan. Slowly heat them together, stirring constantly, until the sugar melts and stops feeling grainy on the bottom of the pan. Turn up the heat and fast-boil until a small amount of mixture dropped into a glass of cold water sets into a soft ball that you can pick up on a teaspoon. The bubbles in the mixture will look small and even.

2 Turn off the heat and keep stirring for 5 minutes or until the mix starts to thicken a little. Sprinkle in the chocolate and swirl it through the mixture once, using a spatula or the handle of a wooden spoon. Pour into a tin and leave the fudge overnight to set, then turn out and cut into squares. Will keep for up to 2 months in an airtight container.

PER SERVING 444 kcals, protein 2g, carbs 54g, fat 26g, sat fat 15g, fibre none, sugar 53g, salt 0.08g

Mint chocolate truffles

This recipe uses milk chocolate but you can use dark if you prefer, or why not make some of each so everyone is happy?

TAKES 35 MINUTES, PLUS CHILLING
● **MAKES ABOUT 20**

100ml/3½fl oz double cream
200g/7oz milk chocolate, broken into
    pieces
¼ tsp peppermint essence
icing sugar, for rolling

1 Bring the cream just to the boil in a pan. Turn off the heat and stir in the chocolate. Stir until melted, then add the peppermint essence. Cool, then chill until the mixture is solid, about 2–3 hours.

2 Scoop out teaspoons of the mixture and roll into small walnut-sized balls with your hands, then roll them in icing sugar. The truffles will keep, chilled, for 3 days, or freeze for up to 1 month.

PER TRUFFLE 81 kcals, protein 1g, carbs 7g, fat 9g, sat fat 3g, fibre none, sugar 7g, salt 0.02g

Coconut ice squares

Here's an old-fashioned favourite that even small kids can make, as there's no cooking involved. Tie the sweets up in squares of muslin or Cellophane to gift wrap.

TAKES 25 MINUTES, PLUS SETTING
● **MAKES ABOUT 30 SQUARES**
50g/2oz sweetened condensed milk
250g/9oz icing sugar, sifted, plus extra
    for dusting
200g/7oz desiccated coconut
a little pink edible food colouring

1 Using a wooden spoon, mix together the condensed milk and icing sugar in a large bowl. It will get very stiff. Work the coconut into the mix until it's well combined – use your hands, if you like.

2 Split the mixture into two and knead a very small amount of food colouring into one half. Dust a board with icing sugar, then shape each half into a smooth rectangle and put one on top of the other. Roll with a rolling pin, re-shaping with your hands every couple of rolls, until you have a rectangle of two-tone coconut ice about 3cm thick.

3 Transfer to a plate or board and leave to set, uncovered, for at least 3 hours or ideally overnight. Cut into squares with a sharp knife and pack into bags or boxes. These will keep for up to a month at least, if stored in an airtight container.

PER SQUARE 79 kcals, protein 1g, carbs 10g, fat 4g, sat fat 4g, fibre 1g, sugar 9g, salt none

Really enormous chocolate buttons

These are simple enough for children to make, and provide perfect presents for granny and grandpa. Younger children will need help melting the chocolate.

TAKES 1 HOUR • MAKES 10 OF EACH KIND

100g/4oz milk chocolate, melted
100g/4oz dark chocolate, melted
100g/4oz white chocolate, melted
a few sprinkles and sweets,
   to decorate

1 Tear off some large sheets of baking parchment. Draw around a glass with a pencil to make big button shapes. Turn the paper over.

2 Spoon a blob of melted chocolate into the middle of each circle and use a clean paintbrush to spread it to the edges of the circle. Don't worry if it isn't neat.

3 Decorate each button with sprinkles, sweets or blobs of other coloured chocolate.

4 Leave the buttons to cool and set really hard. Once they are hard, peel them off the paper carefully and pop them into a Cellophane bag to give as a gift.

PER AVERAGE BUTTON 52 kcals, protein 1g, carbs 6g, fat 3g, sat fat 2g, fibre none, sugar 6g, salt 0.02g

Snowball truffles

These truffles look really special but are a doddle to make. They taste just as scrumptious made with milk chocolate.

TAKES 25 MINUTES, PLUS CHILLING
● **MAKES 30**

200ml/7fl oz double cream
200g/7oz good-quality dark chocolate
   (at least 70% cocoa solids)
200g/7oz desiccated coconut, to coat

1 Pour the cream into a pan and bring it just up to the boil. Chop the chocolate into small pieces and put in a large bowl. Pour over the boiling cream, then stir until the chocolate and cream are well blended and smooth. Cool, then set aside in the fridge until the mixture is solid, about 2 hours.

2 Scoop out teaspoons of the mixture and roll into small walnut-sized balls with your hands. Sprinkle the coconut on to a plate and roll the truffles in the coconut until evenly covered. These truffles will keep in a cool place for 3 days or you can freeze them for up to 1 month.

PER TRUFFLE 111 kcals, protein 1g, carbs 4g, fat 10g, sat fat 7g, fibre 1g, sugar 2g, salt 0.01g

Chocolate truffles

Beautifully wrapped in boxes, these truffles will put a smile on anyone's face. They're very satisfying to make and, best of all, you can make and freeze them ahead.

TAKES 30 MINUTES, PLUS CHILLING

● **MAKES 50**

300g/10oz good-quality dark chocolate (70% cocoa solids), chopped

284ml pot double cream

50g/2oz unsalted butter

FOR FLAVOURING & COATING (OPTIONAL)

a dash bourbon, Grand Marnier, coconut rum or the zest and juice of an orange

a few crushed shelled pistachio nuts, some toasted desiccated coconut or a little cocoa powder

100g/4oz milk, dark or white chocolate (enough for 10 truffles), melted

1 Tip the chocolate into a large bowl. Heat cream and butter gently in a pan until the butter melts and the cream reaches simmering point. Remove from the heat, then pour this over the chocolate, stirring until you have a smooth mixture. Either leave the truffles plain, or divide the mixture among bowls and mix in liqueurs or other flavourings, a teaspoon at a time, to taste. Cool and chill for at least 4 hours.

2 Dip a melon baller in hot water and scoop up balls of the mixture, then drop the truffles on to greaseproof paper or lightly coat your hands in sunflower oil and roll them between your palms. Tip the chosen coatings (pistachio, coconut or cocoa) into bowls and gently roll the truffles in them until evenly coated. Put on greaseproof paper and set aside to chill. Alternatively, you can dip some truffles into melted chocolate.

3 Store in the fridge in an airtight container for 3 days, or freeze for up to a month (defrost in the fridge overnight).

PER TRUFFLE 67 kcals, protein 1g, carbs 3g, fat 6g, sat fat 3g, fibre none, sugar 2g, salt none

Homemade marzipan thins

It takes a while for the icing to dry, so don't stamp out these sweets too soon or you'll end up with fingerprints on the icing.

TAKES 25 MINUTES, PLUS SETTING

● **MAKES ABOUT 80**

200g pack ground almonds
200g/7oz golden caster sugar
200g/7oz golden icing sugar, plus extra
  for dusting
1 egg, beaten
few drops almond essence

TO ICE AND DECORATE

175g/6oz royal icing mix
2–3 tbsp lemon juice
small crystallised fruits

1 Make the marzipan: mix the almonds and sugars until well combined. Add the egg and almond essence, and mix to a stiff paste, using your hands to press the mixture together. Knead briefly on a surface dusted with icing sugar then roll out to a 1cm thickness.

2 Line a baking sheet with baking parchment and carefully set the marzipan on top. Leave to set for 1 hour. Beat together the royal icing and lemon juice, and spread evenly over the marzipan. Leave overnight to dry.

3 Cut the iced marzipan with small cutters and press a piece of crystallised fruit into the centre of each. Pack the marzipan thins into boxes interleaved with baking parchment.

PER THIN 48 kcals, protein 1g, carbs 9g, fat 2g, sat fat 0.1g, fibre 0.2g, sugar 8g, salt 0.01g

Fruit & nut chocolate chequers

These homemade chocs are perfect for a special Valentine, a treat for mum on Mother's Day or simply a small gift for a good friend. They will keep for a week.

TAKES 40 MINUTES, PLUS SETTING
● **MAKES 16 OF EACH FLAVOUR**
FOR THE WHITE CHOCOLATES
150g/5½oz white chocolate
1 tbsp dried raspberry flakes
16 toasted almonds, halved
8 pecan nut halves
8 pinches cocoa powder, for dusting
FOR THE DARK CHOCOLATES
150g/5½oz dark chocolate
1 tbsp candied peel
1 tbsp dried cranberries or raisins, chopped
8 sugared cashews

1 Roughly chop the chocolates, keeping the white and the dark chocolate pieces separate. Line two baking sheets with baking parchment.

2 Melt the chocolates in two heatproof mixing bowls over pans half-filled with water set over a gentle heat. Remove from the heat. Using a teaspoon, spoon the melted chocolates on to the paper in round shapes as evenly as possible – you need 16 of each type of chocolate. Leave a teaspoon of white chocolate in the bowl for later.

3 Chop the raspberry flakes, then scatter them over half the white rounds and top each with two almond halves. Put a pecan on the rest, then swirl over a little of the white chocolate left in the bowl. Sprinkle with cocoa.

4 Scatter half the dark rounds with the candied peel and the other half with the cranberries or raisins and cashews. Leave the chocolates to set and harden for about 3 hours, then pack into a box.

PER CHOCOLATE 259 kcals, protein 4g, carbs 29g, fat 15g, sat fat 7g, fibre 1g, sugar 27g, salt 0.07g

Raspberry–almond bites

If you don't have four baking sheets, make and cook half the quantity, then repeat. These pretty, pink melt-in-the-mouth treats are just right for a girly get-together.

TAKES 50 MINUTES • MAKES 20

4 egg whites
300g/10oz icing sugar
pink or red food colouring
140g/5oz ground almonds
4–5 tbsp raspberry jam
½ × 250g tub mascarpone

1 Whisk the egg whites in a large, clean bowl until soft peaks form. Whisk in the sugar in four batches, whisking well between each addition. Add a couple of drops of colouring. Keep whisking until the mixture is light pink, with no streaks, and is thick and glossy.

2 Using a large metal spoon, gently fold through the ground almonds. Cover four baking sheets with baking parchment. Use four spoons to make 40 circles of mixture, each 5cm wide. Leave to sit for 10 minutes until a skin starts to form.

3 Heat oven to 180C/160C fan/gas 4. Put the baking sheets in the oven, leaving the door slightly ajar to allow steam to escape, then bake for 20–25 minutes until just crisp, but not browned. Leave to cool.

4 Gently ease off the paper using a palette knife. Take half the biscuits and spread 1 teaspoon of the jam over each, and put 1 teaspoon of the mascarpone per biscuit over the rest, then sandwich the two halves together.

PER BITE 140 kcals, protein 2g, carbs 19g, fat 7g, sat fat 2g, fibre 1g, sugar 18g, salt 0.06g

Chocolate macaroons

Weigh and measure your ingredients carefully when making these as the proportions really matter. They are a great little treat when nothing but a chocolate hit will do.

TAKES 45 MINUTES ● **MAKES 12**

125g/4½oz icing sugar
1 tbsp cocoa powder
100g/4oz ground almonds
2 medium egg whites

FOR THE FILLING

50g/2oz milk or dark chocolate, chopped
2 tsp skimmed milk, warmed a little

1 Heat oven to 180C/160C fan/gas 4. Line a large baking sheet with baking parchment. Sift the icing sugar and cocoa into a bowl, then stir in the almonds. Whisk the egg whites until stiff, then fold them into the dry ingredients.

2 Fill an icing bag fitted with a plain nozzle with the mixture (or put it in a large food bag and snip off the corner). Pipe 24 small blobs, about 3cm across, on to the baking sheet, leaving space between each. Smooth the surface with a wet finger, then leave for 15 minutes to dry out. Bake for 15–20 minutes until the macaroons feel firm and peel easily off the paper. Cool on the paper, then peel off and store in a tin for up to 1 week.

3 Put the chocolate into a heatproof bowl and gently melt it over a pan of simmering water. Stir in the milk until smooth. Leave to thicken a little, then use the filling to sandwich the macaroons together.

PER MACAROON 119 kcals, protein 3g, carbs 14g, fat 6g, sat fat 1g, fibre 1g, sugar 14g, salt 0.04g

Chocolate–chestnut cupcakes

Look out for foil cake cases to make these cupcakes look really special as a present.
They will keep in the fridge for 4 days.

TAKES 1 HOUR ● MAKES 18

FOR THE CAKES

435g can chestnut purée
6 eggs
175g/6oz golden caster sugar
200g/7oz ground almonds
1 tsp baking powder

FOR THE TOPPING AND DECORATION

200g/7oz dark chocolate, broken into
   pieces
generous knob butter
400ml/14fl oz double cream
chocolate curls, to decorate
icing sugar and cocoa powder,
   for dusting

1 Line one and a half muffin trays with 18 pretty muffin cases. Heat oven to 180C/160C fan/gas 4. Tip the chestnut purée into a large bowl and mash with a fork. Whisk the eggs and sugar with an electric hand whisk until pale and frothy.

2 Fold half the egg mixture into the chestnut purée to lighten it, then fold in the almonds and baking powder. Gently fold in the rest of the egg, then spoon the batter into the muffin cases. Bake for 25–30 minutes until firm. Leave to cool.

3 To make the chocolate topping, gently melt the chocolate, butter and cream together in a small pan. Pour into a bowl and leave to cool. Beat well to thicken the mixture then swirl it generously on to the cupcakes and pile on chocolate curls. Dust half the cupcakes with icing sugar and the other half with cocoa before serving.

PER CAKE 392 kcals, protein 7g, carbs 31g, fat 28g, sat fat 12g, fibre 2g, sugar 25g, salt 0.27g

Nutty chocolate crunch

This recipe is a great way of turning nuts, biscuits and chocolate into a delicious chocolatey treat. A really scrummy gift from your kitchen.

TAKES 25 MINUTES, PLUS CHILLING
- **CUTS INTO 20 SQUARES**

250g/9oz assorted biscuits, roughly chopped
250g/9oz assorted nuts or a mix of nuts and dried fruit
300g/10oz milk or dark chocolate (or a mixture of both), chopped
100g/4oz butter, chopped
140g/5oz golden syrup

1 Butter and line a 20cm-square baking tin with non-stick baking parchment. In a large bowl, combine the biscuits and nuts or mixed nuts and fruits, halving any larger nuts. Melt the chocolate, butter and golden syrup in a bowl set over a pan of simmering water, stirring occasionally until smooth and glossy, then pour this over the biscuit and nut mixture.

2 Tip the mixture into the tin, then flatten lightly – it doesn't need to be completely smooth. Chill for at least 2 hours or overnight before cutting into small squares.

PER SERVING 267 kcals, protein 5g, carbs 24g, fat 18g, sat fat 7g, fibre 1g, sugar 18g, salt 0.27g

White-chocolate spotty cake

If you want something scrumptious to take along to a coffee morning or to sell at the school fair, these chocolatey sponges fit the bill.

TAKES 50 MINUTES • CUTS INTO 15 SQUARES

250g pack butter, softened, plus extra
for greasing
300g/10oz self-raising flour
250g/9oz golden caster sugar
½ tsp baking powder
4 eggs
150g pot natural yogurt
3 tbsp milk
1 tsp vanilla paste
200g bar white chocolate, half of it
chopped
100g/4oz icing sugar, sifted
300g/10oz soft cheese, not fridge cold
a few sweets, to decorate

1 Heat oven to 180C/160C fan/gas 4. Grease a 20 x 30cm tin, then line with baking parchment. Beat the butter, flour, sugar, baking powder, eggs, yogurt, milk and vanilla until lump-free. Stir in the chopped chocolate. Spoon into the tin and bake for 25–30 minutes until golden and risen, and a skewer comes out clean. Cool in the tin.

2 Melt the rest of the chocolate in a heatproof bowl set over a pan of simmering water. Stir the icing sugar into the soft cheese, then stir in the chocolate until smooth. Chill the frosting, spread over the cake, then cut into squares and decorate with sweets.

PER SQUARE 489 kcals, protein 8g, carbs 55g, fat 28g, sat fat 16g, fibre 1g, sugar 40g, salt 0.73g

Chocolate & caramel flapjacks

Flapjacks are best baked in advance as the base will be stickier after a day. These make a good gift for a teatime treat or are perfect to sell at a charity fundraiser.

TAKES 1 HOUR 5 MINUTES, PLUS COOLING • CUTS INTO 12 MINI SQUARES

200g/7oz light brown soft sugar
200g/7oz butter, plus extra for greasing
2 tbsp golden syrup
350g/12oz whole oats
397g can caramel (we used Carnation Caramel)
200g/7oz dark chocolate
1 tbsp unflavoured oil, such as sunflower

1 Heat oven to 150C/130C fan/gas 2. Put the sugar, butter and golden syrup together in a pan and gently heat until the butter has melted, stirring occasionally. Take the pan off the heat and stir in the oats, mixing thoroughly. Pour the mixture into a lined and lightly greased 22cm-square tin, pressing it out evenly using the back of a wooden spoon. Bake in the centre of the oven for 40–45 minutes.

2 Allow the mixture to cool in the tin for 10 minutes (or, for best results, leave to cool completely overnight), then evenly spread over the caramel. Chill until firm.

3 Melt the chocolate in a heatproof bowl over a pan of barely simmering water, then stir in the oil and pour over the chilled caramel flapjack base. Let the chocolate set, then cut into squares.

PER SERVING 492 kcals, protein 8g, carbs 67g, fat 23g, sat fat 13g, fibre 4g, sugar 48g, salt 0.37g

Cherry & coconut Florentines

These cute, chewy bites are an easy take on the classic Florentine, but with no fiddly shaping. They make a beautiful gift for an after-dinner treat with coffee.

TAKES 50 MINUTES, PLUS CHILLING
- **MAKES 24**

140g/5oz light muscovado sugar
100g/4oz clear honey
200g/7oz salted butter
100g/4oz desiccated coconut
140g/5oz flaked almonds
300g/10oz glacé cherries, sliced
4 tbsp plain flour
250g/9oz dark, milk or white chocolate, or a mix, to ice

1 Heat oven to 200C/180C fan/gas 6. Put the sugar, honey and butter in a large pan and gently melt together. When all the sugar has dissolved, stir in the coconut, almonds, cherries and flour.

2 Line a large baking sheet (about 40 x 30cm) with baking parchment, and roughly spread the Florentine mixture out to a thin layer – don't worry if you have small gaps, it should melt together in the oven. Bake for 10–12 minutes until a rich golden colour, then set aside to cool and firm up.

3 Melt the chocolate(s) all in separate heatproof bowls over gently simmering water. Line a second large baking sheet or board with baking parchment and carefully flip the cooled Florentine bake on to it. Peel off the parchment. Spread the chocolate over – if you're using a few types, just leave a gap between each one. Leave to set, then stamp out shapes using star cookie cutters.

PER SERVING (24) 247 kcals, protein 2g, carbs 26g, fat 15g, sat fat 9g, fibre 1g, sugar 25g, salt 0.15g

Mini macaroons

There are three flavours of mini macaroons from which to choose here and each set of ingredients makes 30, so just decide which you'd like to make for a pretty gift.

TAKES 25 MINUTES PER FLAVOUR, PLUS DRYING ● MAKES ABOUT 30 OF EACH FLAVOUR

PISTACHIO & CHOCOLATE
140g/5oz pistachio nuts
250g/9oz icing sugar
2 egg whites
100g/4oz low-fat soft cheese
25g/1oz dark chocolate (70% cocoa solids), melted

CHOCOLATE
140g/5oz ground almonds
225g/8oz icing sugar
25g/1oz cocoa powder
2 egg whites
100g/4oz low-fat soft cheese
½ tsp instant coffee, dissolved in a few drops boiling water

VANILLA
140g/5oz ground almonds
250g/9oz icing sugar
seeds from 1 vanilla pod
2 egg whites
a little dulche de leche

1 Heat oven to 160C/140C fan/gas 3. For Pistachio macaroons, whizz the nuts and 25g/1oz of the sugar in a processor. Mix with 175g/6oz more sugar in a large bowl. Whisk the egg whites until stiff, add the remaining sugar and whisk again until thick. Fold into the nut mix. Spoon into a piping bag and pipe 10p-coin-size blobs on to lined baking sheets. Leave to dry for 30 minutes, then bake for 12–15 minutes until risen. Cool. Beat the soft cheese with the chocolate and use to sandwich together the macaroons.

2 For Chocolate, mix the almonds with 175g/6oz icing sugar and cocoa. Whisk the whites until stiff, add the remaining sugar and whisk again. Fold into the nut mix and pipe, and cook as above. For the filling, mix the soft cheese with the coffee.

3 For Vanilla, mix the almonds with 200g/7oz icing sugar and the vanilla seeds. Whisk the whites until stiff, add the remaining sugar and whisk again. Fold into the nut mix and pipe, and cook as above. Sandwich with dulce de leche.

PER SERVING 71 kcals, protein 2g, carbs 10g, fat 3g, sat fat 1g, fibre none, sugar 10g, salt 0.05g

Polka-dot caramel shortbread

Ready-made caramel sauce, called dulce de leche, makes these shortbread bakes easy for the kids to make for friends. It is available in jars or cans from supermarkets.

TAKES 40 MINUTES, PLUS CHILLING

● **MAKES 16 PIECES**

140g/5oz plain flour
50g/2oz caster sugar
100g/4oz butter, cold and cubed
50g/2oz chocolate chips

FOR THE FILLING

400g jar dulce de leche

FOR THE TOPPING

100g bar milk chocolate, melted

1 Line a deep 20cm-square baking tin with baking parchment. Sift the flour and sugar together into a bowl, then add the butter and rub in.

2 Stir in the chocolate chips. Tip the mixture into the tin, then press down with the back of a spoon to make an even layer. Chill for 15 minutes. Heat oven to 160C/140C fan/gas 3.

3 Bake the shortbread for about 20 minutes until golden brown. When cool, spoon the dulce de leche caramel over and spread out evenly. Pour the melted chocolate over the caramel. Cool, then cover with cling film and chill well before cutting into triangles. Will keep in an airtight container for up to 3 days.

PER SERVING 208 kcals, protein 3g, carbs 30g, fat 9g, sat fat 5g, fibre none, sugar 20g, salt 0.18g

Tutti-frutti rounds

No baking is required for this irresistible recipe. Just chop up some dried fruits, crush some biscuits and mix them into melted white chocolate and butter.

TAKES 20–30 MINUTES, PLUS CHILLING
● **MAKES ABOUT 32**

200g bar white chocolate (Belgian is ideal), broken into pieces
125g/4½oz butter, cut into pieces
6 rich tea biscuits or 12 rich tea fingers
4 green glacé cherries (or angelica), rinsed and chopped
50g/2oz dried cranberries
2 tbsp raisins

1 Tip the chocolate and butter into a large microwave-proof bowl. Microwave on Medium for about 3 minutes, stirring once, until melted, or set the bowl over a pan of simmering water and stir the chocolate and butter until melted. Set aside to cool.

2 Put the biscuits in a large freezer bag and crush with a rolling pin – they should have some crunch left in them. Stir the biscuits and all the fruits into the melted chocolate. Chill for 2 hours until they are almost solid.

3 Lay a sheet of cling film on a work surface. Scoop out half of the chilled mixture on to the cling film. Roll into a sausage the diameter of a £2 coin. Repeat with remaining mixture. Chill overnight. The rolls can be chilled for up to 3 days or frozen for up to 2 months.

4 Unwrap each roll and cut into 16 rounds. To give as presents, arrange the rounds in pretty boxes.

PER ROUND 76 kcals, protein 1g, carbs 7g, fat 5g, sat fat 2g, fibre none, sugar 3g, salt 0.11g

Chocolate chunk–pecan cookies

There's something very decadent about American-style cookies with their chunks of chocolate and nuts. Use a good-quality chocolate with 70 per cent cocoa solids.

TAKES 30 MINUTES ● MAKES 12

200g/7oz dark chocolate, broken into squares
100g/4oz butter, chopped
50g/2oz light muscovado sugar
85g/3oz golden caster sugar
1 tsp vanilla extract
1 egg, beaten
100g/4oz whole pecan nuts
100g/4oz plain flour
1 tsp bicarbonate of soda

1 Heat oven to 180C/160C fan/gas 4. Melt 85g/3oz of the chocolate in a microwave-proof bowl in the microwave on High for 1 minute or over a pan of simmering water.

2 Beat in the butter, sugars, vanilla and egg until smooth, then stir in three-quarters of both the nuts and the remaining chocolate, then the flour and bicarbonate of soda.

3 Heap 12 spoonfuls, spaced apart, on two baking sheets (don't spread the mixture), then poke in the reserved nuts and chocolate. Bake for 12 minutes until firm, then leave to cool on the sheets. Can be stored in a tin for up to 3 days.

PER COOKIE 294 kcals, protein 4g, carbs 27g, fat 20g, sat fat 8g, fibre 2g, sugar 17g, salt 0.44g

Chunky chocolate–nut bars

Here's a scrumptious, spicy idea for chocolate and nut lovers. Wrap the shortbread bars prettily as gifts. Will store for a week in an airtight tin.

TAKES 50–60 MINUTES, PLUS SETTING
● **MAKES 44**

200g/7oz chilled salted butter, cut into small pieces, plus extra for greasing

325g/11oz plain flour

2 tsp ground cinnamon

125g/4½oz golden caster sugar

2 tsp vanilla extract

2 egg yolks

400g/14oz luxury mixed whole nuts

175g/6oz dark chocolate, broken into pieces, to drizzle

175g/6oz milk chocolate, broken into pieces, to drizzle

1 Heat oven to 180C/160C fan/gas 4. Grease two shallow 28 × 18cm baking trays and line with greaseproof paper to come above the rim of the tin. Grease the paper.

2 Tip the flour and cinnamon into a food processor. Add the butter, then whizz to breadcrumbs. Add the sugar, vanilla and egg yolks, and whizz to a smooth dough. Pack half the dough into each tin, pressing it into the corners. Scatter evenly with nuts, pressing them into the dough.

3 Bake for 40 minutes until golden. Carefully lift out of the tins, still on the paper, and transfer to a wire rack to cool.

4 Melt the chocolates in separate bowls over pans of simmering water. Leaving the biscuit slabs on the paper, cut each slab widthways into 2cm slices. Drizzle lines of dark chocolate over them, using a dessertspoon, then drizzle milk chocolate over the dark. Leave to set. Cut each biscuit in half widthways to serve.

PER BISCUIT 173 kcals, protein 3g, carbs 14g, fat 12g, sat fat 5g, fibre 1g, sugar 7g, salt 0.1g

Coconut & chocolate macaroons

To crack open a fresh coconut, wrap it in a cloth to keep it steady, then give it a hefty whack with a hammer. That should do the trick.

TAKES 50 MINUTES ● MAKES 12

1 egg white
200g/7oz caster sugar
4 tbsp plain flour
200g/7oz coarsely grated fresh
    coconut, about 1 coconut in total
150g bar dark chocolate, chopped,
    to ice

1 Heat oven to 180C/160C fan/gas 4. In a clean bowl, whisk the egg white until stiff then gradually add the sugar, whisking continuously until thick and glossy. Sift in the flour, then fold it in with the coconut until completely combined.

2 Using an 8cm pastry cutter, squash spoonfuls of the mixture on to a baking sheet lined with non-stick baking parchment – you may need to do this in two batches. Bake for 15–18 minutes until golden around the edges and just starting to brown on top. Leave to cool, then transfer to a wire rack.

3 While the macaroons are cooling, melt the chocolate in a microwave or over a pan of simmering water and leave to cool slightly. Cover the smooth side with chocolate and leave to set in the fridge. The macaroons will keep in an airtight container for 2 days.

PER SERVING 206 kcals, protein 2g, carbs 30g, fat 10g, sat fat 7g, fibre 2g, sugar 26g, salt 0.03g

Double choc shortbreads

The children will love helping you ice these with their friends' names to take to a special birthday party.

TAKES 45 MINUTES • MAKES 25

200g/7oz butter, cubed
325g/11oz plain flour, plus extra for
    rolling
100g/4oz caster sugar
1 tsp vanilla extract
2 egg yolks
100g/4oz dark or milk chocolate chips
200g bar white chocolate, melted,
    to ice
red writing icing tube, to decorate

1 Rub the butter into the flour to make crumbs, then stir in the sugar, vanilla, yolks and chocolate chips, and bring together to form a dough. Roll out on a lightly floured surface and stamp out 6cm-round biscuits. Re-roll the trimmings and repeat. Arrange on parchment-lined baking sheets and chill for 30 minutes.

2 Heat oven to 200C/180C fan/gas 6. Bake the biscuits for 10–12 minutes until golden. Cool. Spread each with white chocolate and leave to set. Decorate with friends' names and leave to set.

PER SERVING 192 kcals, protein 2g, carbs 22g, fat 11g, sat fat 6g, fibre none, sugar 12g, salt 0.12g

Triple chocolate cookies

If these cookies look a little under-done after their cooking time, they're probably perfect. Keep a batch of unbaked dough in the freezer ready to finish when needed.

TAKES 25 MINUTES ● MAKES 24

100g/4oz light brown soft sugar
100g/4oz golden caster sugar
100g/4oz butter, softened
1 egg
1 tsp vanilla extract
225g/8oz plain flour
140g/5oz milk chocolate, melted
85g/3oz white chocolate, chips or
    chopped into chunks
85g/3oz dark chocolate, chips or
    chopped into chunks

1 Heat oven to 200C/180C fan/gas 6. Line one or two baking sheets with baking parchment. Mix the sugars and butter together with a wooden spoon, then add the egg, vanilla, flour and half the melted milk chocolate, and mix together. Stir in the white and dark chocolate chips or chunks, then use an ice-cream scoop or round tablespoon (like a measuring spoon) to scoop out balls of cookie dough and drop them straight on to the baking sheets.

2 Bake in batches for 8–9 minutes until pale golden and still soft to the touch – they will firm up as they cool. Carefully transfer to a wire rack as soon as they can be lifted up, then drizzle them with the remaining melted chocolate.

PER COOKIE 167 kcals, protein 2g, carbs 24g, fat 8g, sat fat 5g, fibre none, sugar 17g, salt 0.1g

Fudgy coconut brownies

Rich, dense and gooey, these easy-to-make brownies are the perfect present for a coffee morning. The coconut gives them a fabulous texture.

TAKES 1 HOUR • CUTS INTO 16 SQUARES

100g/4oz cocoa powder
250g/9oz butter
500g/1lb 2oz golden caster sugar
4 eggs, beaten
100g/4oz self-raising flour
100g/4oz desiccated coconut

1 Heat oven to 180C/160C fan/gas 4. Line the base of a 20cm-square baking tin with baking parchment. Put the cocoa, butter and sugar in your largest pan and gently melt, stirring so the mixture doesn't catch. When the cocoa mixture is melted and combined, cool slightly, then stir in the eggs, little by little, followed by the flour and coconut.

2 Tip into the tin and bake for around 45 minutes on a middle shelf – check after 30 minutes and cover with another piece of baking parchment if the crust is browning too much. Cool in the tin, then carefully lift out and cut into squares.

PER BROWNIE 358 kcals, protein 3g, carbs 43g, fat 21g, sat fat 13g, fibre 2g, sugar 35g, salt 0.39g

Treacle tart hearts

Make something special and show your loved one you really care on Valentine's day with a homemade sweet heart.

TAKES 45 MINUTES, PLUS CHILLING
● **MAKES 8**

FOR THE PASTRY

200g/7oz cold unsalted butter, cubed

350g/12oz plain flour, plus extra for rolling out

½ tsp ground ginger

100g/4oz golden caster sugar

1 egg yolk

FOR THE FILLING

400g/14oz golden syrup

finely grated zest 1 lemon and juice of ½

100g/4oz fine white breadcrumbs

1 Blitz the butter, flour and ginger in a food processor to fine crumbs. Stir in the sugar, then add the egg yolk and 2 teaspoons cold water. Pulse until the dough clumps together. Turn out on to a floured surface and press into a smooth round. Chill until firm.

2 Roll out the pastry to the thickness of two £1 coins and stamp out eight 11cm circles (or cut around a saucer and trim to fit the tins). Line eight 10cm width heart-shaped tins with pastry. Re-roll the trimmings. With a small cutter, stamp out eight hearts. Chill the tins and hearts for 15 minutes. Heat oven to 180C/160C fan/gas 4 and heat a baking sheet.

3 Stir together the syrup, lemon zest and juice. Divide the breadcrumbs among the tins, then spoon the syrup over slowly, adding more when it has soaked in. Top with the small pastry hearts. Bake on the hot baking sheet for 25 minutes until the pastry is golden and the filling is slightly set. Serve just warm.

PER SERVING 452 kcals, protein 5g, carbs 78g, fat 16g, sat fat 10g, fibre 2g, sugar 47g, salt 0.59g

Cherry shortbread hearts

Indulge the special person in your life by cooking something homemade and delicious for Valentine's day. Box up these biscuits for an irresistible gift.

TAKES 30 MINUTES ● MAKES 14–16

100g/4oz icing sugar, plus extra for dusting

200g/7oz plain flour, plus extra for dusting

50g/2oz cornflour

50g/2oz ground almonds

250g pack cold butter, cut into cubes

50g/2oz glacé cherries, finely chopped

½ tsp almond extract

8 tbsp cherry jam, sieved

1 Heat oven to 180C/160C fan/gas 4. Sift the icing sugar, flour and cornflour together into a bowl. Stir in the ground almonds and butter, then rub in the butter until smooth. Stir in the chopped glacé cherries and almond extract, and bring together to form a dough.

2 Roll out on a lightly floured surface, then stamp out biscuits using a heart-shaped cutter. Keep re-rolling the trimmings until all the dough is used. Carefully transfer the biscuits to baking sheets lined with baking parchment and bake for 8–10 minutes until they are just pale golden.

3 Using an upturned bottle top or similar, press gently into the centre of each biscuit to make a round indent. Spoon in a little jam and return to the oven for 2 minutes. Remove and cool on a wire rack, before dusting with icing sugar to serve.

PER SERVING (16) 242 kcals, protein 2g, carbs 27g, fat 15g, sat fat 8g, fibre 1g, sugar 14g, salt 0.21g

Simple chocolate-button egg

You can use milk or white chocolate for this egg, depending on your preference. You'll need a chocolate-egg mould.

TAKES ABOUT 30 MINUTES, PLUS DRYING ● MAKES 1 EGG

FOR THE EGG

200g/7oz good-quality dark chocolate, broken into pieces

TO DECORATE

25g bag white chocolate buttons

25g bag white chocolate speckled buttons

1 Melt the dark chocolate in a heatproof bowl set over a pan of simmering water. Stir until smooth, then leave until cool. Spoon a quarter of the chocolate into a chocolate-egg mould and spread it thickly and evenly over the inside with a pastry brush. Be sure to cover the sides well. Leave in a cool place to set, then chill in the fridge for 5 minutes.

2 Re-warm the remaining dark chocolate and repeat the process for each side of the mould, reserving 1 tablespoon of chocolate. Use a knife to scrape away any excess around the rim of the mould to give a clean, straight edge. Turn out each half on to greaseproof paper, carefully pulling away the mould.

3 Put one half of the egg on its back. Warm the reserved chocolate and brush it around the edge of the egg. Put the other egg half on top and press together. Leave in a cool place to set firm. Dab a little chocolate on the backs of the white chocolate buttons and press them on to the egg to decorate.

PER ¼ EGG 172 kcals, protein 2g, carbs 16g, fat 12g, sat fat 6g, fibre 2g, sugar 11g, salt 0.01g

Chilli chocolate-egg lollies

An Easter indulgence for the grown-ups. Add the chilli powder gradually, tasting as you go. You could make some spotty milk-chocolate lollies without the chilli for the kids.

TAKES 30 MINUTES, PLUS SETTING
- **MAKES 10–12**

140g/5oz dark chocolate, broken into
    pieces
2–3 pinches hot chilli powder
12 lolly sticks
edible red glitter or sprinkles,
    to decorate

1 Draw an egg shape about 6cm long on a piece of paper, and use as a template to draw about 10–12 shapes on sheets of baking parchment. Hole-punch a piece of paper a bit bigger than the egg shape, to make a polka-dot stencil. (By folding the paper in half, you can get holes right to the middle of it.)

2 Melt the chocolate in a bowl over a pan of barely simmering water. Stir in the chilli (taste to check heat), then spread a spoon or two of chocolate inside each egg shape. Add a lolly stick to each. Hold the stencil just over the wet surface of one of the lollies and stick into place with Blu-Tack, but don't let it touch. Sprinkle edible glitter or sprinkles over, then gently lift off the stencil. Repeat to decorate the rest, then leave somewhere cool to set.

PER LOLLY 61 kcals, protein 1g, carbs 8g, fat 3g, sat fat 2g, fibre none, sugar 8g, salt none

Chocolate–fudge Easter cakes

Look out for gold- or pastel-coloured paper cake cases to make these chocolate treats look extra pretty at Easter. These are easy enough for the kids to make with you.

TAKES 30 MINUTES • MAKES 16

FOR THE CAKES

140g/5oz soft butter

140g/5oz golden caster sugar

3 medium eggs

100g/4oz self-raising flour

25g/1oz cocoa powder, sifted

FOR THE FROSTING

85g/3oz milk chocolate, broken into pieces

85g/3oz soft butter

140g/5oz icing sugar, sifted

FOR THE DECORATION

2 × 35g packs white chocolate Maltesers

mini foil-wrapped chocolate eggs

1 Heat oven to 190C/170C fan/gas 5 and put 16 cases into bun tins. Tip all the ingredients for the cakes into a mixing bowl and beat for 2 minutes with an electric hand whisk until smooth. Divide the mixture among the cake cases so they are two-thirds filled, then bake the cakes for 12–15 minutes until risen. Cool on a wire rack.

2 For the frosting, microwave the chocolate in a bowl on High for 1 minute. Cream the butter and sugar together, then beat in the melted chocolate. Spread on the cooled cakes and decorate with Maltesers and mini chocolate eggs.

PER SERVING 274 kcals, protein 3g, carbs 31g, fat 16g, sat fat 9g, fibre 1g, sugar 25g, salt 0.43g

Cherry & almond Easter cupcakes

The marzipan adds a delicious almondy flavour and texture to these easy-to-make cupcakes. The perfect Easter present for family or friends.

TAKES 1 HOUR • MAKES 24

250g pack butter, softened
175g/6oz golden caster sugar
5 eggs, beaten
250g/9oz self-raising flour, plus an
    extra 2 tbsp for dusting
1 tsp baking powder
zest 1 orange, plus 2 tbsp of the juice
200g/7oz glacé cherries, halved
250g/9oz natural marzipan, coarsely
    grated (easiest if chilled
    beforehand)
½ tsp almond essence

FOR THE ICING AND DECORATION

175g/6oz icing sugar, sifted
mini chocolate eggs

1 Heat oven to 180C/160C fan/gas 4. Arrange 24 paper cake cases in bun tins. Beat the butter and sugar together with electric beaters until light and fluffy. Add the eggs, flour, baking powder, orange zest and juice, and beat well until thick and evenly mixed.

2 Toss the cherries in the extra 2 tablespoons flour and fold into the batter along with the grated marzipan and almond essence. Divide among the cake cases and bake for 20–25 minutes until well risen and golden. Leave the cakes to cool in the tins for 10 minutes, then turn out on to a wire rack to cool completely.

3 Mix the icing sugar with just enough cold water to make a loose but not-too-runny icing. Spread over the cakes and top with the chocolate eggs.

PER CAKE 267 kcals, protein 3g, carbs 39g, fat 12g, sat fat 6g, fibre 1g, sugar 30g, salt 0.34g

Sugar-dusted wedding cookies

An English shortbread-based version of the classic Mexican cookie. Preserving sugar is perfect for adding crunch, but if you can't get hold of it just use demerara.

TAKES 50–60 MINUTES ● MAKES ABOUT 60–70

250g/9oz salted butter, softened
140g/5oz caster sugar
1 egg, separated, plus 2 egg yolks
2 tsp vanilla extract
100g/4oz ground rice
300g/10oz plain flour
140g/5oz preserving sugar

1 In a large bowl, mix the butter, caster sugar, three yolks and vanilla with a wooden spoon until creamy. Stir in the ground rice and flour – you may need to get your hands in at the end to get all of the dry ingredients incorporated. Roughly divide the mixture into three.

2 Lay out three large sheets of greaseproof paper, and on each one, roll a third of the dough into a long, thin sausage – about 2.5cm thick. Lightly beat the egg white, then brush it all over the dough. Scatter over the preserving sugar and roll the dough so it is completely coated. Wrap up in the paper and transfer to the fridge for 30–40 minutes until firm.

3 Heat oven to 200C/180C fan/gas 6. Using a sharp knife, slice each roll into 20–30 small biscuits. Arrange them over baking parchment-lined baking sheets allowing some space between them – they will spread a little. Bake for 8–12 minutes until pale golden. Cool on the baking sheets until firm.

PER COOKIE 76 kcals, protein 1g, carbs 10g, fat 4g, sat fat 2g, fibre 0.2g, sugar 5g, salt 0.06g

Sugar dusted
wedding cookies

Homemade chocolate drops

A mix of dark, milk and white chocolate drops, prettily decorated and presented in pastel-coloured boxes, make perfect wedding favours.

TAKES 1¼ HOURS ● MAKES ABOUT 200, ENOUGH FOR 20–40 FAVOURS

FOR DARK CHILLI DROPS

200g/7oz dark chocolate (70% cocoa solids)

pinch hot chilli powder

sprinkling of edible red glitter, to decorate

FOR SALTED PISTACHIO DROPS

200g/7oz milk chocolate

⅛ tsp flaky sea salt

25g/1oz pistachio nuts, finely chopped

FOR ROSE DROPS

200g/7oz white chocolate

a few crystallised rose petals

1 For the dark chilli drops, break the chocolate into chunks and melt in a heatproof bowl over a pan of barely simmering water. Meanwhile, line a few baking sheets with baking parchment. Once the chocolate has melted, stir in the chilli powder. Use a teaspoon to drop 'drops' of the chocolate on to the baking parchment. Every 10 or 20 drops, scatter over a small amount of red glitter before the chocolate sets. Leave to set in a cool place, but do not put in the fridge.

2 For the salted pistachio drops, melt the chocolate and prepare the baking sheets as before. Once the chocolate has melted, stir in the salt, then make drops as above, topping with the pistachios.

3 For the white chocolate drops, carefully melt the chocolate as above and make the drops as before. Once they are partially set, top each with a crystallised rose petal.

PER FAVOUR (20) 167 kcals, protein 2g, carbs 19g, fat 10g, sat fat 5g, fibre 0.4g, sugar 19g, salt 0.09g

Summer spice mix

Whole spices keep their flavour much longer than ground spices and look prettier, too. These party or wedding favours can double up as place-names on the table.

TAKES 5 MINUTES ● MAKES ENOUGH FOR 8–10 SMALL BAGS

25g/1oz black peppercorns
50g/2oz fennel seeds
50g/2oz coriander seeds
50g/2oz cumin seeds
2 tbsp brown or white mustard seeds
2 tbsp crushed chillies

1 Simply mix all the spices together in a bag or large bowl. You can make up the mix and pack it into individual bags a month before the celebration.

2 Attach a label with these instructions: 'Transfer the mix to a peppermill and use it to grind over meat, fish or veg before barbecuing, or straight into curries.'

PER BAG (8) 95 kcals, protein 4g, carbs 10g, fat 5g, sat fat 0.2g, fibre 0.1g, sugar none, salt 0.05g

Peppermint lollipops

These are fun for a wedding or a party. Put the lollies in a container anchoring them in sugar, or package individually in Cellophane, with ribbon tied around the stick.

TAKES 50 MINUTES • MAKES ABOUT 40

500g/1lb 2oz granulated sugar
1 tsp cream of tartar
200ml/7fl oz hot water
2 tsp peppermint essence
a few drops of green food colouring
40 plastic lollipop sticks, or wooden skewers cut into short lengths

1 Put the sugar and cream of tartar into a pan with the hot water. Gently heat until the sugar has completely melted, then increase the heat and boil until the mixture reaches the 'hard crack' stage on a sugar thermometer (or a small spoonful dropped into cold water sets hard). Remove from the heat immediately and swirl in the peppermint essence and enough green colouring to give a pale green colour – start by adding just one drop at a time.

2 Cover a heatproof surface with baking parchment. Using a metal spoon, carefully pour some peppermint syrup on to the paper – roughly ½–1 tablespoon per lolly. Push a lolly stick into each. If the syrup becomes too thick, just put the pan back over a gentle heat briefly; but if the syrup is too hot and runny, the shapes won't be as even, so set the pan aside for a minute. Leave the lollies to set until hard.

PER LOLLY 50 kcals, protein none, carbs 13g, fat none, sat fat none, fibre none, sugar 13g, salt 0.07g

Lavender sugar

These mini jars of flavoured sugar look really pretty, tied with pastel ribbon, and make unusual homemade wedding favours that won't break the bank.

TAKES 1 MINUTE ● MAKES ENOUGH TO FILL 8–10 SMALL BAGS OR JARS
1kg/2lb 4oz caster sugar
2 tsp lavender flowers, picked (or buy in jars)

1 Mix the sugar and lavender, then divide among small bags or jars up to 2 months before the big day.

2 Attach a label with these instructions: 'Use the flavoured sugar within 6 months. It's great in shortbread, sprinkled over a sponge or stirred into summer berries.'

PER JAR (8) 494 kcals, protein none, carbs 132g, fat none, sat fat none, fibre none, sugar 132g, salt 0.02g

Lavender sugar

Treat to shortbread, sprinkle over a
orange or stirred into berries
Use within 6 months

Malloween ghosts

Made with melted marshmallows, these little cakes are both chewy and crisp.
Why not pop them into a black box to take to a Halloween party?

TAKES 50 MINUTES • MAKES 18

100g/4oz unsalted butter, plus a little
 extra for the tin
300g/10oz pink and white
 marshmallows
200g/7oz puffed rice cereal
300g/10oz white chocolate, melted, for
 coating
a little melted dark chocolate or black
 writing icing, to decorate
18 wooden lolly sticks or coffee stirrers
 (stirrers are a little more bendy)

1 Butter then line a 30 × 20cm Swiss roll tin with baking parchment. Melt the butter in a large non-stick pan, tip in the marshmallows and melt very gently for about 10 minutes, stirring regularly to make sure they don't stick.

2 Once smooth, stir in the cereal until coated. Spoon the mixture into the tin, then press down to make it flat. Chill until set.

3 Cut the cake into rectangles, then use a sharp knife to round off the tops of each and zig-zag the bottoms so they look like ghosts.

4 Carefully push a lolly stick into the bottom of each ghost. Put on to a wire rack. Spoon over the white chocolate and paint it over and down the sides of the ghosts with a pastry brush. Leave to set. Pipe on eyes with the dark chocolate or black icing.

PER GHOST 233 kcals, protein 3g, carbs 35g, fat 10g, sat fat 6g, fibre none, sugar 22g, salt 0.24g

Spooky spider cakes

These spider cakes make a great centrepiece for a Halloween party. You could give each child a plain cake and let them decorate their own, with a small prize for the best.

TAKES 1 HOUR ● MAKES 12

200g/7oz butter, at room temperature
200g/7oz golden caster sugar
200g/7oz self-raising flour
4 eggs
½ tsp baking powder
1 tsp vanilla extract
6 tbsp chocolate chips or chopped
    chocolate

TO DECORATE

2 packs liquorice Catherine wheels
12 tbsp chocolate spread
a few liquorice allsorts (the black ones
    with the white centre)
1 length red bootlace
tube black writing icing

1 Heat oven to 180C/160C fan/gas 4 and line a muffin tin with 12 cases. Put the butter, sugar and flour in a mixing bowl. Add the eggs, baking powder and vanilla, then beat with an electric hand whisk until smooth and creamy. Stir in the chocolate. Spoon the cake mixture evenly into the cases and bake for 20–25 minutes until golden – a cocktail stick pushed into the cakes should come out clean. Cool on a wire rack.

2 Unravel the liquorice wheels and cut into 96 lengths with scissors to make dangly legs. Stick eight into the top of each cake, making small cuts in the sponge with a sharp knife so the legs push in securely.

3 Spoon the chocolate spread on top, within the liquorice legs, to make a spider's body. Cut the allsorts to make eyes and red bootlaces to make mouths, then stick them on to the cakes and dot on icing to make eyeballs.

PER SERVING 481 kcals, protein 6g, carbs 63g, fat 24g, sat fat 10g, fibre 1g, sugar 45g, salt 0.64g

Squeamish squares

These will be a big hit to take to any Halloween party – sticky, crunchy and chewy in one bite. They will keep in an airtight container for up to 2 days.

TAKES 20 MINUTES, PLUS CHILLING
- **MAKES 16 SQUARES OR 32 BITE-SIZED CHUNKS**

150g bar dark chocolate, broken into pieces (70% cocoa solids)

100g/4oz unsalted butter

4 tbsp golden syrup

100g/4oz puffed rice cereal

50g/2oz dried blueberries

50g/2oz dried cranberries

100g/4oz mini marshmallows

TO ICE AND DECORATE

50g/2oz white chocolate, broken into pieces

a few jelly snakes and bugs

1 Line a 20cm-square baking tin with baking parchment or cling film. Place the dark chocolate, butter and syrup in a pan over a low heat and stir until melted.

2 Put the rice cereal in a large bowl and mix in the blueberries, cranberries and marshmallows. Stir in the melted chocolate mixture until everything is well coated. Spoon the mixture into the tin and spread out evenly. Chill in the fridge for an hour until set (or make the day before and chill overnight).

3 Remove from the tin and peel away the paper or cling film. Using a sharp knife, cut into 16 squares or 32 bite-sized pieces. Melt the white chocolate in a small bowl over a pan of barely simmering water, or in the microwave on High for 1 minute, stirring halfway through. Using a teaspoon, drizzle the white chocolate over the squares. Scatter with the jelly sweets, then allow to set before serving.

PER SERVING 197 kcals, protein 2g, carbs 26g, fat 10g, sat fat 6g, fibre 1g, sugar 17g, salt 0.15g

Monster cupcakes

Children will love decorating these cakes to make their own monsters. The perfect spooky gift for a Halloween teatime party.

TAKES 35 MINUTES ● MAKES 12

FOR THE CAKES

250g/9oz self-raising flour
25g/1oz cocoa powder
175g/6oz light muscovado sugar
85g/3oz unsalted butter, melted
5 tbsp vegetable or sunflower oil
150g pot fat-free natural yogurt
1 tsp vanilla extract
3 eggs

FOR THE FROSTING AND DECORATION

85g/3oz unsalted butter, softened
1 tbsp milk
½ tsp vanilla extract
200g/7oz icing sugar, sifted
a selection of food colourings (optional)
a few sweets and sprinkles

1 Heat oven to 190C/170C fan/gas 5 and line a 12-hole muffin tin with deep cake cases. Put all the cake ingredients into a large bowl and beat together with an electric whisk until smooth. Spoon the mixture into the cases, then bake for 20 minutes until risen and a skewer inserted into the middle comes out dry. Cool completely on a wire rack. The cakes can be made up to 3 days ahead and kept in an airtight container, or frozen for up to 1 month.

2 For the frosting, work the butter, milk and vanilla into the icing sugar until creamy and pale. Colour with food colouring, if using, then create your own gruesome monster faces using sweets and sprinkles. See who can make the scariest face!

PER FROSTED CAKE 389 kcals, protein 5g, carbs 53g, fat 19g, sat fat 9g, fibre 1g, sugar 36g, salt 0.3g

Homemade toffee apples

Nothing beats the crunch of a homemade toffee apple on an autumnal evening.
Pack these up for a surprise treat at a Bonfire Night get-together.

TAKES 20 MINUTES • MAKES 8

8 Granny Smith apples
400g/14oz golden caster sugar
1 tsp vinegar
4 tbsp golden syrup
8 lolly sticks

1 Put the apples in a large bowl and cover with boiling water. Dry them thoroughly and twist off any stalks. Push a lolly stick into the stalk end of each apple.

2 Lay out a sheet of baking parchment and put the apples on this. Tip the sugar into a pan with 100ml 3½fl oz water and cook over a medium heat for 5 minutes until the sugar dissolves, then stir in the vinegar and syrup. Set a sugar thermometer in the pan and boil to 140C/284F or 'hard crack' stage. Or test the toffee by pouring a little into a bowl of cold water – it should harden instantly and, when removed, be brittle. If you can still squish the toffee, continue to boil it.

3 Working quickly and carefully, dip and twist each apple in the toffee until covered. Let any excess drip away, then put them on parchment to harden. Heat the toffee a little if it starts to feel thick. Leave to cool before eating.

PER SERVING 278 kcals, protein none, carbs 73g, fat none, sat fat none, fibre 2g, sugar 73g, salt 0.06g

Campfire cupcakes

If you've been invited to a Guy Fawkes Night party, bake a batch of these cupcakes to take along, then simply top them with marshmallows and flash them under the grill.

TAKES 30 MINUTES • MAKES 12

140g/5oz light muscovado sugar
100g/4oz self-raising flour
50g/2oz cocoa powder
1 tsp baking powder
3 eggs
125ml/4fl oz vegetable oil
3 tbsp milk
50g/2oz milk chocolate chips
30g pack mini marshmallows,
    to decorate

1 Heat oven to 180C/160C fan/gas 4. Tip the sugar, flour, cocoa and baking powders into a large bowl. In a separate bowl, whisk together the eggs, oil and milk, then stir together with the dry ingredients until well combined. Add the milk chocolate chips. Put cupcake cases into a 12-hole bun tin, divide the mixture among the cases, then bake for 20 minutes until risen and cooked through. You can now leave them to cool and store for up to 2 days in an airtight container, if you wish.

2 Just before serving, arrange the marshmallows over the tops of the cakes. Heat grill to medium and pop the cakes under it for 30 seconds, watching them all the time and cooking only until the marshmallows are lightly browned. Remove and eat straight away.

PER SERVING 233 kcals, protein 3g, carbs 25g, fat 14g, sat fat 3g, fibre 1g, sugar 16g, salt 0.27g

Baked Camembert kit

Melted Camembert served with crusty bread is always a treat, and here's a special kit to give as a gift to a friend – remind them to keep it in the fridge.

TAKES 20 MINUTES, PLUS COOLING

● **SERVES 2**

100g/4oz sultanas

5 tbsp calvados, PX sherry, rum or brandy

1 boxed Camembert

TO COMPLETE THE KIT

small jar

string or ribbon

label

1 Heat the sultanas and alcohol together until just simmering, then turn off the heat and leave to cool completely. Spoon into a small jar and seal. Put the jar on top of the cheese and tie together with string or ribbon.

2 Keep in the fridge for up to a week until you are ready to give them away, then add a label with these instructions: 'Heat oven to 200C/180C fan/gas 6. Unwrap the Camembert, take off the wax wrapper and any other packaging. Put it back in the box but leave the lid off. Cook for 10 minutes or until the centre of the cheese feels very soft. Cut a slashed cross in the centre of the cheese then tip in and over as many of the sultanas as you like. Serve with chunks of crusty bread.'

PER SERVING 618 kcals, protein 28g, carbs 44g, fat 29g, sat fat 19g, fibre 1g, sugar 44g, salt 1.95g

Baked
Camembert
with Marinated
Sultanas

Apricot Stilton pots

If you wish, the potted Stilton can be packaged up with some oatcakes or other crisp savoury biscuits to make an attractive festive gift.

TAKES 10–15 MINUTES ● MAKES 3

300g/10oz Stilton
100g/4oz softened butter
40g/1½oz chopped walnuts
25g/1oz dried apricots, chopped

1 Crumble or grate the Stilton into a small bowl. Beat the softened butter until creamy, then stir in the Stilton.
2 Pack into three 150ml ramekins and smooth the tops. Mix the walnuts and apricots, and press them on top of the cheese. Wrap in cling film and chill for up to a week or freeze for up to 2 months.

PER POT 766 kcals, protein 26g, carbs 4g, fat 72g, sat fat 41g, fibre 1g, sugar 4g, salt 2.42g

Spanish fig & almond balls

This is a festive version of pan de higo, a dried fig cake that the Spanish traditionally eat with cheese. Wrap in Cellophane and present with some crackers and cheese.

TAKES 20 MINUTES, PLUS DRYING
- **MAKES 6**

100g/4oz whole almonds, toasted
500g pack dried whole figs, hard stalk and centre of base removed
85g/3oz dried apricots, chopped into small pieces
50g/2oz dried cranberries
1 tbsp brandy
1 tbsp clear honey
1 tsp ground cloves
100g/4oz sesame seeds, toasted, to coat

1 Whizz the almonds in a food processor until most are finely chopped, then tip into a large bowl. Roughly chop the figs, then whizz to a smooth, sticky paste. Scrape on to the almonds then, using your hands, mix together well with the remaining dried fruit, brandy, honey and cloves.

2 Divide the mixture into six and roll into balls. Tip the sesame seeds on to a baking sheet, then roll the balls in them until covered. Cover the baking sheet loosely with a clean tea towel, then leave the fig balls to dry for a week before packaging. Will keep in a cool place for 2 months. Serve with cheese and a drizzle of honey.

PER BALL 306 kcals, protein 8g, carbs 24g, fat 20g, sat fat 2g, fibre 5g, sugar 23g, salt 0.05g

Snowflake cakes

Orange blossom water is a popular Middle Eastern ingredient used to add a citrus–floral flavour to bakes or savoury dishes. It's available from supermarkets and delis.

TAKES 55 MINUTES • MAKES 10

125g/4½oz softened butter, plus extra
    for greasing
140g/5oz self-raising flour
125g/4½oz golden caster sugar
½ tsp baking powder
2 eggs
½ × 150g pot natural yogurt
zest 1 clementine
3 tbsp orange blossom water
icing sugar, to dust

1 Heat oven to 180C/160C fan/gas 4. Line ten holes of a muffin tin with cases (or grease some snowflake cake moulds).

2 Beat the butter, flour, sugar, baking powder, eggs, yogurt, clementine zest and 2 tablespoons of the orange blossom water in a large bowl with an electric whisk until lump-free. Spoon into the cases (or fill the cake moulds three-quarters full), and bake for 18–22 minutes until golden and risen – a skewer poked in should come out clean (check the cake moulds after 15 minutes).

3 Drizzle with the remaining orange blossom water while warm, then cool. Dust with icing sugar to serve.

PER SERVING 290 kcals, protein 4g, carbs 33g, fat 16g, sat fat 10g, fibre 1g, sugar 19g, salt 0.5g

Mini panettone

You don't need to buy special tins to make these, just save up 200g-size cans (baked beans etc), or use ten holes of a muffin tin, lined with muffin wraps, instead.

TAKES 1¼ HOURS, PLUS RISING
● **MAKES 10**

2 eggs, plus 1 yolk
1 tsp vanilla paste or extract
500g/1lb 2oz plain flour
2 × 7g sachets easy-blend dried yeast
100g/4oz caster sugar
½ tsp salt
200ml/7fl oz warm milk
200g/7oz soft butter
140g/5oz mixed dried fruit
100g/4oz mixed candied peel
milk, for brushing
1–2 tbsp flaked almonds, for scattering

1 Beat the eggs and yolk with the vanilla. In a large bowl, mix the flour, yeast, sugar and salt. Add the warm milk and egg mixture, then beat to a very soft, sticky dough with a wooden spoon. Cover with cling film and leave in a warm place until the dough has roughly doubled in size.

2 Drop large muffin wraps into ten clean 200g-size cans (or use a muffin tray), or line them with baking parchment so that the paper comes well above the rim of the cans, to make a collar.

3 Blend the butter, fruit and peel into the risen dough, preferably with your hands. Cut into ten equal pieces and drop a piece into each prepared can. Cover again and leave until well risen.

4 Heat oven to 190C/170C fan/gas 5. Gently brush the panettone with milk, scatter over the almonds and bake for 25–30 minutes until golden. Eat within 3 days, or freeze for up to 6 weeks.

PER PANETTONE 472 kcals, protein 9g, carbs 71g, fat 20g, sat fat 11g, fibre 2g, sugar 30g, salt 0.65g

Spiced & iced Christmas trees

Kids will love making – and receiving – these biscuit lollies. Any leftover dough can be used to make mini star biscuits.

TAKES 1¼ HOURS • MAKES 16 PLUS EXTRA STARS

FOR THE BISCUITS

100g/4oz butter, chopped
175g/6oz dark muscovado sugar
85g/3oz golden syrup
350g/12oz plain flour, plus extra for
    dusting
1 tbsp ground ginger
¼ tsp ground cloves
1 tsp ground cinnamon
1 tsp bicarbonate of soda
1 egg, beaten

TO ICE AND DECORATE

300g/10oz sifted icing sugar
16 lolly sticks
a few sweets

1 Gently melt the butter, muscovado sugar and syrup in a large pan until the sugar dissolves. Mix together the flour, spices and ½ teaspoon salt. Cool the butter mixture a little, then stir in the bicarbonate of soda. Immediately add half the spiced flour and beat well. Add the egg and remaining spiced flour, then beat to make a soft dough. Tip on to a sheet of foil, flatten to a large disc and chill until firm.

2 Heat oven to 190C/170C fan/gas 5. Roll out half the dough on a floured surface. Stamp out trees using a cutter about 10cm long and arrange, well spaced apart, on baking sheets. Bake for 12–15 minutes until golden. Leave to harden. Repeat with the remaining dough. Use the trimmings to stamp out 3–4cm stars and bake for 9–10 minutes.

3 Mix about 3 tablespoons water into the icing sugar to make icing. Use to sandwich two trees together with a lolly stick between them, then use the rest to decorate, along with some sweets.

PER TREE 278 kcals, protein 3g, carbs 57g, fat 6g, sat fat 3g, fibre 1g, sugar 39g, salt 0.47g

Classic mincemeat

This is rich with dark treacley sugar, fresh and dried fruits and a more than generous glug of whisky. Make some for you and some to give away.

TAKES 30 MINUTES • MAKES ABOUT 4 × 450ML/16FL OZ JARS

1 medium Bramley apple
300g/10oz raisins
300g/10oz currants
300g/10oz shredded suet (use
   vegetarian, if you prefer)
250g/9oz dark muscovado sugar
85g/3oz chopped mixed peel
grating nutmeg
pinch ground mixed spice
finely grated zest and juice 1 lemon
   and 1 small orange
100ml/3½fl oz whisky
4 fresh bay leaves

1 Peel and grate the apple and set aside. Mix together all the ingredients, except the apple, whisky and bay leaves, in the order they are listed.

2 Stir through the apple, then add the whisky once all the other ingredients are completely combined.

3 To sterilise the jars, wash them thoroughly in hot soapy water, rinse, and then dry in a low oven. Make sure you leave the jars to cool completely before filling or the suet will melt.

4 Tuck a bay leaf into each jar to scent the mincemeat, then seal. Leave for 2 weeks before using. Will keep for 6 months.

PER TBSP 93 kcals, protein none, carbs 13g, fat 4g, sat fat none, fibre none, sugar 12g, salt 0.02g

Festive jammie dodgers

Everyone loves jammie dodgers and this Christmassy version is sure to be a welcome present for family or friends.

TAKES 50 MINUTES • MAKES 24

225g/8oz unsalted butter, softened
100g/4oz caster sugar
200g/7oz plain flour, plus extra for
    dusting
100g/4oz ground almonds
100g/4oz strawberry or raspberry jam
    (about ½ jar)

1 Whizz the butter, sugar, flour and almonds in a food processor until the mixture forms a ball. Wrap in cling film and chill for 1 hour.

2 Knead the dough until soft enough to shape, then divide into two equal balls. Roll out one ball on a lightly floured work surface to a 5mm thickness. Using a star cutter (about 6cm wide) dipped in flour, cut out as many star shapes as you can. Re-roll the trimmings and cut out more stars until you have about 24. Put the stars on a baking sheet, keeping them spaced apart.

3 Roll out the second ball of dough. Cut out same-size stars and put them on a baking sheet. Now cut out and discard a small circle in the centre of 24 biscuits using the end of a large piping nozzle.

4 Heat oven to 140C/120C fan/gas 1 and cook the biscuits for 20–30 minutes until golden. Cool on a wire rack. Put a generous blob of jam on to the centre of the biscuits without the cut-out circles. Top with the remaining biscuits.

PER BISCUIT 151 kcals, protein 2g, carbs 14g, fat 10g, sat fat 5g, fibre 1g, sugar 8g, salt 0.01g

Lebkuchen

These traditional German biscuits are a favourite at Christmas. They taste a bit like gingerbread, with a chewy centre and a hint of seasonal spices.

TAKES 30 MINUTES ● MAKES 30

250g/9oz plain flour

85g/3oz ground almonds

2 tsp ground ginger

1 tsp ground cinnamon

1 tsp baking powder

½ tsp bicarbonate of soda

pinch each ground cloves, grated nutmeg and freshly ground black pepper

200ml/7fl oz clear honey

85g/3oz butter

finely grated zest 1 lemon

FOR THE ICING

100g/4oz icing sugar

1 egg white, beaten

1 Tip the dry ingredients into a large bowl. Heat the honey and butter in a pan over a low heat until the butter melts, then pour into the flour mixture along with the lemon zest. Mix well until the dough is combined and fairly solid. Cover and leave to cool.

2 Heat oven to 180C/160C fan/gas 4. Using your hands, roll the dough into about 30 balls, each 3cm wide, then flatten each one slightly into a disc. Divide the biscuits between two baking trays lined with baking parchment, leaving room for them to expand. Bake for 15 minutes, then transfer to a wire rack to cool.

3 To ice the biscuits, mix together the icing sugar, egg white and 1–2 tablespoons water to form a smooth, runny icing. Dip the top of each biscuit in the icing and spread with the back of a knife. Leave to dry in a warm place. Store in an airtight tin for up to a week.

PER BISCUIT 102 kcals, protein 2g, carbs 16g, fat 4g, sat fat 2g, fibre 0.5g, sugar 9g, salt 0.16g

Triple-chocolate cupcake kit

Here's a clever idea for a chocoholic friend – put together the ingredients along with this recipe for baking a batch of wickedly tempting cupcakes.

TAKES 25 MINUTES ● MAKES 1 KIT TO BAKE 12 CUPCAKES

100g/4oz golden caster sugar
100g/4oz self-raising flour
2 tbsp cocoa powder

TO COMPLETE THE KIT

large glass jar with a clip or screw lid
200g/7oz white chocolate drops
100g/4oz bar milk chocolate or drops
Cellophane, ribbon, gift bag or box and
    large label
1 new spatula or wooden spoon
a few edible sprinkles, or other
    decorations
12 cupcake cases

1 Tip the caster sugar into the jar, followed by the flour, then finally the cocoa, so the ingredients sit in layers. Seal the jar.

2 Wrap up the chocolate drops separately in Cellophane. Tie the spatula or spoon on to the jar with ribbon and pack in a gift bag or box with the chocolates, sprinkles and the cupcake cases.

3 Hand-write a label with the following instructions and attach it to the gift: 'Heat oven to 180C/160C fan/gas 4. Put 100g/4oz very soft butter in a bowl with two eggs, add the contents of the jar and beat well. Add a drop of milk to the mixture if it is too stiff. Stir in the white chocolate drops. Divide among the cake cases. Bake for 15 minutes. Cool. Melt the milk chocolate, spoon a little over each cake and then decorate them with sprinkles.'

PER CUPCAKE 202 kcals, protein 3g, carbs 31g, fat 9g, sat fat 5g, fibre none, sugar 24g, salt 0.15g

Triple chocolate cupcakes

Christmas brownie lollipops

It's best to avoid using brownies with large nut or chocolate pieces for the lollipops as this will make it hard to roll them into balls.

TAKES 17 MINUTES, PLUS COOLING
- **MAKES 24**

300g/10oz nut-free brownies
50g/2oz chocolate, finely chopped
100ml/3½fl oz single cream
a few edible sprinkles, to decorate
24 lolly sticks or wooden coffee stirrers

1 Cut the brownies into 24 pieces, then use your hands (greasing them if necessary) to roll each piece into a little ball about the size of a truffle. Insert a lolly stick, or wooden coffee stirrer snapped in half, into each ball.

2 Put the chocolate into a large bowl. Bring the cream just to the boil in a small pan, then pour the hot cream over the chocolate. Leave for a few minutes until starting to melt, then stir until smooth. Dip the brownie lollipops into the melted chocolate until coated all over, scatter over the sprinkles to decorate, then leave for 30 minutes until set. Try inserting the lolly sticks into an empty egg box to allow them to cool upright. Can be made up to 2 days in advance and stored in a cool place.

PER LOLLIPOP 78 kcals, protein 1g, carbs 8g, fat 5g, sat fat 3g, fibre none, sugar 7g, salt 0.06g

Christmas cupcakes

These cupcakes are a joy to make with kids – the recipe is incredibly easy to follow and, as they include chocolate buttons, they're sure to be a hit.

TAKES 45 MINUTES ● MAKES 12

FOR THE CAKES

300g/10oz self-raising flour
175g/6oz golden caster
175g/6oz unsalted butter, very soft
150g pot fat-free natural yogurt
1 tsp vanilla extract
3 eggs

FOR FROSTING

85g/3oz unsalted butter, softened
1 tsp vanilla extract
200g/7oz icing sugar, sifted

TO DECORATE

natural green food colouring
    (for Christmas trees), sweets,
    sprinkles and white chocolate
    stars
milk and white chocolate buttons
natural food colouring icing pens

1 Heat oven to 190C/170C fan/gas 5 and line a 12-hole muffin tin with cake cases. Put all the cake ingredients in to a bowl and mix with a whisk until smooth. Spoon the mixture into the cases, bake for 25 minutes until golden and risen and a skewer inserted into the centre comes out clean. Cool on a wire rack.

2 For the frosting, beat the butter, vanilla extract and icing sugar until pale and creamy and completely combined.

3 To make snowmen, reindeer and Christmas puddings, first spread the frosting over the top of each cake. Then lay the chocolate buttons on top, slicing some buttons into quarters to make ears and hats. Finally, use icing pens for the details. For the Christmas trees, colour the icing with green food colouring and pipe on to the cakes using a star-shaped nozzle, decorate with sweets, sprinkles and white chocolate stars.

PER CUPCAKE 408 kcals, protein 5g, carbs 53g, fat 20g, sat fat 12g, fibre 1g, sugar 36g, salt 0.31g

Double-ginger gingerbread men

Even the smallest hands can help to make these friendly little fellows. You can also use raisins, sultanas or Smarties to decorate, if you prefer.

TAKES 1 HOUR • MAKES 12 BIG GINGERBREAD MEN

140g/5oz unsalted butter
100g/4oz dark muscovado sugar
3 tbsp golden syrup
350g/12oz plain flour
1 tsp bicarbonate of soda
2 tsp ground ginger
1 tsp ground cinnamon
pinch cayenne pepper (optional)
pinch salt
2 balls stem ginger from a jar, chopped

TO DECORATE

50g/2oz icing sugar
a few glacé cherries (we used undyed)
2 balls stem ginger

1 Heat oven to 200C/180C fan/gas 6. Line two baking sheets with baking parchment. Melt the butter, sugar and syrup in a pan. Mix the flour, bicarbonate of soda, spices and salt in a bowl. Stir in the butter mix and ginger to make a stiff-ish dough.

2 When cool enough to handle, roll out the dough to about 5mm thick. Stamp out gingerbread men, re-rolling the dough and cutting out more men. Lift on to the baking sheets. Bake for 12 minutes until golden. Cool for 10 minutes, then lift on to wire racks to cool.

3 Mix the icing sugar with a few drops of water until thick. Halve then slice the cherries thinly to make smiles, and cut the ginger into small squares. Spoon the icing into a food bag, snip off the tiniest corner, then squeeze eyes and buttons and a tiny smile on to one man at a time. Stick on a cherry smile and ginger buttons. Repeat and leave them to set. Will keep for 1 week in an airtight tin.

PER SERVING 264 kcals, protein 3g, carbs 43g, fat 10g, sat fat 6g, fibre 1g, sugar 20g, salt 0.33g

Cranberry & white chocolate panettone

The hands-on time for making this is short, so you just need to be patient as you wait for the dough to rise. Will keep for 2 weeks wrapped in foil.

**TAKES 3 HOURS 50 MINUTES,
INCLUDING RISING ● CUTS INTO
8 SLICES**

500g/1lb 2oz plain flour, plus extra for rolling

2 × 7g sachets easy-blend dried yeast

1 tsp salt

100g/4oz golden caster sugar

3 eggs

1 tsp vanilla extract

200ml/7fl oz milk, warmed to hand hot

200g/7oz butter, softened and cut into pieces, plus extra for greasing

175g/6oz dried cranberries

100g/4oz candied mixed peel, finely chopped

85g/3oz white chocolate, chopped into chunks

TO FINISH

1 egg, lightly beaten

2 tbsp flaked almonds

1 Tip the flour, yeast and salt into a food processor fitted with a dough blade. Mix briefly, then add the sugar and mix again. Beat the eggs with the vanilla. Add the eggs and milk to the dry ingredients and mix to a soft dough. Work the dough in the processor for 2 minutes, then leave in the machine until doubled in size, about 1 hour.

2 Add the butter to the processor and pulse; leave for 1 hour to rise again. Add the cranberries, peel and chocolate, then pulse gently.

3 Butter and base-line a 20cm-deep cake tin. Make a 10cm collar with double thickness of baking paper and line the sides of the tin. Tip out the dough on to a floured surface and quickly knead into a ball. Drop the dough into the tin and leave to rise for 30 minutes. Heat the oven to 180C/160C fan/gas 4.

4 Brush the dough with egg and scatter over the almonds. Bake for 45–50 minutes until deep golden brown. Cool on a wire rack.

PER SERVING 681 kcals, protein 13g, carbs 95g, fat 30g, sat fat 17g, fibre 3g, sugar 44g, salt 0.65g

Fruity Christmas biscotti

These will keep in an airtight tin for up to a month. They make a pretty gift when presented in a seasonal box or a Cellophane bag tied with ribbon.

TAKES 1¼ HOURS ● MAKES ABOUT 72

350g/12oz plain flour, plus extra for rolling
2 tsp baking powder
2 tsp ground mixed spice
250g/9oz golden caster sugar
3 eggs, beaten
coarsely grated zest 1 orange
85g/3oz raisins
85g/3oz dried cherries
50g/2oz blanched almonds
50g/2oz shelled pistachio nuts

1 Heat oven to 180C/160C fan/gas 4. Line two baking sheets with baking parchment. Mix the flour, baking powder, spice and sugar in a large bowl. Stir in the eggs and zest until the mixture starts forming clumps, then bring the dough together, kneading until no floury patches remain. Work the fruit and nuts into the dough.

2 Turn out the dough on to a lightly floured surface and divide into four pieces. With lightly floured hands, roll each piece into a sausage about 30cm long. Put two on each sheet, well spaced apart. Bake for 25–30 minutes until the dough has risen and spread, feels firm but still looks pale. Transfer to a wire rack for a few minutes until cool enough to handle. Turn down oven to 140C/120C fan/gas 1.

3 Using a bread knife, cut the dough into 1cm-thick diagonal slices, then lay on baking sheets. Bake for 15 minutes, turn over, then bake again for another 15 minutes until dry and golden. Cool.

PER BISCUIT 50 kcals, protein 1g, carbs 9g, fat 1g, sat fat none, fibre none, sugar 6g, salt 0.06g

Orange & ginger stained-glass biscuits

The children will love helping to make these magical decorations for the tree. Thread them with ribbon to make a perfect present for Granny.

TAKES 35 MINUTES • MAKES 14

sunflower oil, for greasing
175g/6oz plain flour, plus extra for
    dusting
1 tsp ground ginger
zest 1 orange
100g/4oz cold butter, cut into chunks
50g/2oz golden caster sugar
1 tbsp milk
14 fruit-flavoured boiled sweets
about 120cm thin ribbon, to decorate
icing sugar, to dust

1 Heat oven to 180C/160C fan/gas 4. Grease two large non-stick baking sheets with oil. Whizz the flour, ginger, zest and butter with ½ teaspoon salt to fine crumbs in a food processor. Pulse in the sugar and milk. Turn out and knead briefly on a floured surface until smooth. Wrap in cling film and chill for 30 minutes.

2 Roll out the dough to the thickness of a £1 coin. Use 7cm cutters to cut out shapes, then use 4cm cutters to cut out the middles. Re-roll leftover pieces. Make a hole in the top of each biscuit, then lift on to baking sheets.

3 Crush the sweets in their wrappers with a rolling pin, then put the pieces into the middles of the biscuits – the sweets should be level with the top of the dough. Bake for 15–20 minutes or until the biscuits are golden and the middles have melted.

4 Leave to harden, then transfer to a wire rack to cool. Thread through the holes with ribbon, then dust with icing sugar. Will keep for a month.

PER SERVING 160 kcals, protein 2g, carbs 23g, fat 8g, sat fat 5g, fibre 1g, sugar 10g, salt 0.14g

Sparkling vanilla Christmas cookies

These iced biscuits look a picture hanging from the tree, or packed into pretty boxes as end-of-term gifts for teachers, friends or grandparents.

TAKES 25 MINUTES, PLUS CHILLING
- **MAKES 20**

FOR THE COOKIES

140g/5oz icing sugar, sieved

1 tsp vanilla extract

1 egg yolk

250g/9oz butter, cut into small cubes

375g/13oz plain flour, sieved, plus extra
   for rolling

TO ICE AND DECORATE

200g/7oz icing sugar, sieved

a little edible food colouring

a few gold and silver edible balls

about 2m/6½ft thin ribbon, cut into
   10cm/4in lengths

1 Tip the icing sugar, vanilla, egg yolk and butter into a mixing bowl, then stir together with a wooden spoon (or pulse in a food processor until well combined). Add the flour and mix to a firm dough. Shape the dough into two flat discs and wrap in cling film. Chill for 20–30 minutes. Heat oven to 190C/170C fan/gas 5 and line two baking sheets with non-stick baking parchment.

2 Roll out the dough on a lightly floured surface to the thickness of two £1 coins. Cut out Christmassy shapes and place on baking sheets. Using a skewer, pierce a small hole in the top of each cookie. Bake for 10–12 minutes until lightly golden in colour.

3 Cool the cookies on a wire rack. Meanwhile, mix the icing sugar with a little cold water to make a thick, but still runny, icing and add a colouring of your choice. Spread it over the cooled biscuits, decorate with edible balls and thread with ribbon when dry.

PER SERVING 233 kcals, protein 2g, carbs 34g, fat 11g, sat fat 7g, fibre 1g, sugar 19g, salt 0.2g

Rudolph's snowball carrot muffins

Help your children create a little of their own seasonal magic with these fluffy muffins to leave by the chimney on Christmas Eve for Santa's trusty reindeer!

TAKES 30 MINUTES ● MAKES 12

425g can pineapple in juice
200g/7oz self-raising flour
1 tsp bicarbonate of soda
85g/3oz golden caster sugar
50g/2oz desiccated coconut
2 eggs
85g/3oz butter, melted
150g pot natural bio yogurt
175g/6oz grated carrot

TO ICE AND DECORATE

50g/2oz creamed coconut from
   a sachet
juice from the pineapple can
100g/4oz icing sugar
50g/2oz desiccated coconut
1 tube orange writing icing
a few strips crystallised angelica

1 Heat oven to 200C/180C fan/gas 6 and line a muffin tin with 12 paper cases. Drain the pineapple, reserving the juice, then crush the flesh with a fork. Mix the dry ingredients in a large bowl. Beat the eggs, melted butter and yogurt together and pour into the bowl, along with the carrot and pineapple. Stir quickly, then spoon into muffin cases and bake for 18 minutes or until risen and golden.

2 To decorate, mix the creamed coconut with 5 tablespoons of the reserved pineapple juice and stir in the icing sugar. Put the desiccated coconut on to a plate. Peel the muffins from their cases and put on a wire rack. Spread the icing over until completely covered (this can get a bit messy), then roll in the coconut. Leave to dry for a few minutes. Pipe a carrot on the top of each muffin using the writing icing, with strips of angelica as stalks.

PER MUFFIN 287 kcals, protein 4g, carbs 38g, fat 14g, sat fat 10g, fibre 2g, sugar 25g, salt 0.63g

Chilli vodka

This fun gift takes just a few minutes to prepare and a few hours to steep. Perfect for adding a kick to a Bloody Mary, or just enjoying as it is over ice.

TAKES 5 MINUTES, PLUS MARINATING
● **MAKES 1 LITRE/1¾ PINTS**
2 fat red chillies, plus extra for bottling
1-litre bottle vodka

1 Slice the chillies and mix with the vodka in a large bottle or jug. Leave for 4–5 hours.
2 Strain out the chillies and pour the liquid back into a bottle to store until needed. Just before giving away, decant the vodka into smaller glass bottles, pop a whole chilli in each and label.

PER 25ML/1FL OZ 56 kcals, protein none, carbs none, fat none, sat fat none, fibre none, sugar none, salt none

Index

Also available from BBC Books and *Good Food*

For 6,000 recipes you can trust see bbcgoodfood.com

bbcgoodfood.com

Great-value family food

Nutty chicken curry

Easy weeknight suppers

Easy sweet & sour chicken

Smart entertaining

Sea bass with sizzled ginger, chilli & spring onion

Hundreds of desserts

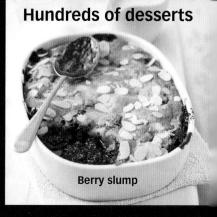

Berry slump

Over 6,000 recipes you can trust